Passage of Tears

THE AFRICA LIST

ABDOURAHMAN
A.WABERI

Passage of Tears

TRANSLATED BY DAVID BALL
AND NICOLE BALL

LONDON NEW YORK CALCUTTA

Series Editor: Rosalind C. Morris

Seagull Books, 2017

First published in Paris as *Passage des Larmes*
by Abdourrahman A. Waberi
© Édition Jean-Claude Lattès 2009

English Translation © David Ball and Nicole Ball, 2011

First published in English translation by Seagull Books, 2011

ISBN   978 0 8574 2 531 7

British Library Cataloguing-in-Publication Data
A catalogue record for this book is available from the British Library

Typeset and designed by Seagull Books, Calcutta, India
Printed and bound by Hyam Enterprises, Calcutta, India

●

For Martina

To the memory of Omar Maalin,
Djiboutian poet

Contents

Acknowledgements

I am grateful for all the support I received during my stay as writer-in-residence (2006–07) in Berlin while I was writing this novel, and particularly for the support of Laura Munoz and Nina Hardt of the Berliner Kunstlerprogramm (DAAD).

I also wish to thank Timothy Peltason, Anjali Prabhu, Lidwien Kapteijns and Mursal Farah Afdub, who gave me invaluable assistance in various ways when I was Susan and Donald Newhouse Fellow in the Humanities at Wellesley College (Massachusetts) in 2007–08.

As far as I know, three writers have used the life of Walter Benjamin as material for their novels: Jay Parini (*Benjamin's Crossing*, 1996); Ricardo Cano Gaviria (*El pasajero Walter Benjamin*, 2000); and Bruno Arpaia (*Dernière Frontière* in the French translation published by Liana Levi in 2002). Although we have taken different routes, I am pleased to find myself in such good company.

Finally, I owe a great deal to the many luminous writers and scholars who have studied the life and work of this singular thinker: Theodor W. Adorno, Hannah Arendt, Stéphane Mosès, Tilla Rudel, Gershom Scholem and Susan Sontag, among others. I also owe much to my friend Tahar Bekri, Tunisian poet and academic, who helped me with the Koranic lexicon.

I am grateful to all of them.

●

The way home is more lovely than home itself.

Mahmoud Darwish

With his soul each person will take his indescribable flight, like the swallow before the storm.

Ossip Mandelstam

I

Devil's Islets

A magnificent indigo body of water that looks like a lake, Goubet al-Kharab (the Devil's Cauldron) is the very end of the Gulf of Tadjoura. The Gulf comes to die not far from Lake Assal and the volcanic zone of Ardoukouba in an impressive setting of arid mountains.

Inside Goubet: Devil's Island (or more exactly Devil's Islets), a former undersea crater. Oyster fossils have been found on its summit.

Such a Long Absence

I've already been back for three days. I returned to Djibouti for professional reasons, not to feast at the table of nostalgia or reopen old wounds. I'm twenty-nine, and I've just signed a contract with a North American company; my remuneration will be substantial. I must hand in the results of my investigation, which will not fail to satisfy its gargantuan appetite: a complete file, with notes, maps, sketches and snapshots, to be delivered to the Denver office asap. I have just under a week to wrap-up the whole thing. I will be paid in Canadian dollars transferred to my account, based in Montreal—like me. After that, I am no longer covered by the company. It will be at my own expense. At my own risk, their legal counsel Ariel Klein repeated to me, frowning with his one long eyebrow, as bushy as Frida Kahlo's. He wished me good luck, turned on his heel and walked away. I headed to the airport with my little trapper's suitcase.

5

So here I am on assignment in the land of my birth, the land that would not or could not keep me. Grieving is not one of my talents, I admit. I don't like goodbyes or returns; I hate all emotional demonstrations. The past interests me less than the future and my time is precious. It has the colour of a greenback. In the world I come from, time doesn't stretch out before you into the mist. Time is money. And money makes the world go round. Money is the stock market, with its flows of pixels, algorithms, figures, commodities, manufactured goods, rating indexes, ideas, sounds, images or simulation models that pop up on screens the world over. It is the life force of the universe, it's about killing the competition and grabbing the coveted market.

I'm back. For a mission neither easier nor harder than any other. For three days now, I've been poking my eyes and ears into everything everywhere, trying to penetrate the mystery of the shadowy manoeuvers that began before I got here. Since that Wednesday, 28 September, when I got a mysterious phone call before my scheduled flight from Montreal to Djibouti via Paris the next day, I've been tracking down tiny clues like a prospecting geologist who never runs out of aquifers and oil wells to drill.

Yesterday, just before I listened to the News at
Five O'Clock from the BBC from London in Somali,
I wrote up my first report:

*Somewhere between Assab and Zeïlah, as you go by
the Gulf of Tadjoura, there is a land without water. A
rocky land, ploughed by the stubborn steps of men. It
sprang up from prehistoric chaos and was once greener
than Amazonia. Since then, the boiling sap of its own fires
has kept the sun from growing old. As for men, they have
been there since the dawn of time, their feet dusty from
walking the powdery earth, their spirits tumbling down
the stones of time. The men of this ancient country have always been waiting for something: a storm, a messiah or an
earthquake. Luckily, there is the fog. A real pea-soup fog
that falls and settles in for the day. Men, ever alert,
have set a trap for the fog. A diabolically clever system:
impressive canvases of seventy square metres—courtesy
of the American military—have been spread out on the
beach on each side of a perimeter as big as a soccer field.
They are not meant to be used by an open-air cinema but
to collect that fog water. The tiny particles floating in the
air are trapped in them; they flow down into a gutter connected to a pipe. The water obtained from this operation
is filtered and its effluvia of hydrocarbon eliminated. It*

tastes good, although rich in sodium and calcium. The fog can produce several litres of water a day, but it is unpredictable by nature. Yet this capricious manna can sometimes meet the daily needs of several families who have been driven from the capital. To the extent that I can rely on appearances, young people here are excellent fog hunters.

NOTEBOOK 1, NOTE 1, under 'Climate'.

This is how I gather my notes; I record my harvest in small dark blue moleskine notebooks numbered 1 to 10. I do hope these notes will help me bring my investigation to a successful conclusion: once they have been assembled, checked, analyzed and compared, a guiding principle will emerge from the sea. A plan will be brought to light. My sponsors will derive maximum benefit from it. The uranium magnates, who are betting on the extinction of oil and the renewed interest in nuclear energy, will put billions of dollars on the table once the battle to restore security has been won. Their mouths are watering over 'this long-neglected region' (I'm quoting the first words of my assignment sheet from memory), 'which has significant uranium potential, judging by its surface and geological profile'.

My mission consists in feeling out the temperature on the ground, making sure the country is secure, the situation stable and the terrorists under control. Intelligence is at the core of the world economy in wartime, its strongest sector, which has been well funded by governments since 9/11. Hundreds of young dynamic companies have entered the field.

These past few years, the Americans are intent on quickly making up for their profound ignorance of the rest of the world. Universities are scrambling to hire professors of Arabic, Persian, Lingala or Turkmen. They're creating new positions to make up for lost time. Of all Washington's activities, intelligence takes precedence. Of course, the companies that have rushed into this sector are not all in military intelligence. Some of them use flocks of translators and speakers of the most obscure languages. They periodically send the CIA and the big military–industrial conglomerates confidential notes that complete the data gathered by the embassies and the usual channels of information in the countries concerned.

Other companies put their cutting-edge capacities at the service of the state and civil defence, for pay. The frantic competition between companies of this new kind does the rest. The little computer whizzes work hand in hand with the brains and hawks of the Pentagon. That's how the biometric signs measuring the physical characteristics unique to each individual—like facial traits, fingerprints or iris scans—are translated into algorithms and inscribed on each passport as barcodes. This technology could not have spread to every point of entry into American territory in so little time without the help of these new companies, like ours— the economic intelligence company Adorno Location Scouting, located in Denver, Colorado.

Our group, which originally specialized in logistics and scouting locations for film shoots, has been able to grow uninterruptedly in the last few years in its market niche. Thousands of federal agents, airline employees and civil defence auxiliaries have done weeks of internships inside similar companies. It's called outsourcing, a practice borrowed from the business world and now used without qualm by most governments. Half the American forces in Iraq are composed of individuals recruited by private agencies. They are not counted in the statistics. Something goes wrong? No casualties to record, no press release.

Everyone does the same thing. The British recently handed over the protection of their embassies and consulates in Kabul, Islamabad, Nairobi and elsewhere to the same organizations. To the same security units, as they say in official jargon.

And here I am in Djibouti, an essential square on the ever-changing geopolitical chessboard. I left in record time with a small suitcase. Objective: intelligence plus profitability. Mobility, discretion and efficiency: the three key words of our group. Needless to say, we do not operate in the open. The group is a past master of deception and simulation.

I am back. I must leave nothing to chance and trust my intuition, for across the centuries and through the rocks, everything here is a sign, everything has meaning. The most banal anecdote may turn out to be the missing piece of the puzzle, the smallest clue leading you to the key you're looking for. The clearest things are often the hardest to grasp. Which reminds me of Poe's story *The Purloined Letter*. I reread it on the plane that brought me here. The detective Auguste Dupin found the letter everyone was looking for, although it was in plain view on the culprit's desk. These things happen more often than you'd think.

I only have a handful of days left to wrap everything up before the weekend. It starts on Thursday, ever since the government changed the calendar fifteen or twenty years ago to show the regional powers how eager it was to join the camp of Allah. The newly decolonized country was thus leaving the Western orbit and its Gregorian calendar to return to its ancestral Muslim fold. Ancestral? Right. No comment.

I must speed up but without rushing it, for this mission isn't a one-man commando operation of the *hit-and-run** kind, as the agents of the Mossad—with whom we have, in fact, excellent relations—would say. I must feel out the temperature and let Nature enter me, permeate my senses, sharpen my cognitive faculties. I can be reached and found 24/7. At every moment, I keep myself ready to report on my mission to my superior, the head of the Global Logistics department, who must be skiing with his nice little family at this very moment.

There's lots of snow in the Rockies, I thought, as I listened distractedly to the grievances of my child-hood friends. They come in bunches, with their arms

---

* All italicized English words are in English in the original.—*Trans.*

12

dangling at their sides and their eyes on the lookout. They want to see me 'after all these years of absence', they say, putting on conspiratorial airs. I know they haven't come to admire my pretty face but to take the measure of a curious object: the native turned Canadian. To wring some money out of me, too, most of the time a two-thousand Djibouti-franc bill, the equivalent of twelve American dollars. Just one won't come and put on this act: my brother Djamal. I haven't seen him since I was eighteen. He's too proud to associate himself with these parasites.

All of them try the economic-refugee number on me. According to them, they all try hard, but they just don't have any luck. They get up at dawn but that doesn't help, what with the favouritism, unemployment, corruption and all the injustice in the world. They all wear the same costume of a sad clown; they love to cry over their own fate. The only right that people here want to exercise is the right to shut up or leave the country as fast as possible. I listen to them with one very distracted ear and keep taking notes for my investigation.

I have a practised eye, an eye that can pick up the slightest detail in the hollow of a face or the depths of a landscape. The small hair sticking out of a nostril or the most banal assemblage of rocks in the brush —nothing must escape my vigilance. There is an impressive number of twisted faces, of people with goitre or tuberculosis. I would never have seen so many in my youth, when my father and mother were still alive. There is more migratory movement in the region; more poverty, too.

I'm paid to scrutinize this country inside out. To record everything, analyze and put it through the scanner if necessary. Every piece of data will be weighed and measured over and over. Photographed every which way. Every shot enlarged a hundred or a thousand times. Sent off instantly to the offices of Adorno Location Scouting. Connected to their agents across the five continents. They stay open 24/7.

●

*Alif**

In the name of Allah the Most Merciful, full of mercy. Praise be to Allah the Lord of Worlds. The Most Merciful, full of mercy, the Master of the Day of Judgement. It is Allah we worship, Allah we implore. Allah, who leads on the paths of righteousness, the path of those upon whom Allah lavishes His blessings, not of those who anger Allah or stray from His path.

O you foreigner, wake up!

Open your ears before it is too late! Open your eyes wide! Look! We know you have returned, you are staying in the big hotel facing the sea. You move around a lot, usually alone. We are watching your every move. We are here, and elsewhere. We are everywhere. We are near you—so near we can feel the muscles of your neck contracting, your jugular

---

* Some chapters bear the names of 16 of the 28 letters of the Arabic alphabet: *Alif, Ba, Ta, Ha, Kha, Dal, Dha, Ra, Zay, Sin, Shin, Sad, Dhad, Ta, Za, Aïn, Gaïn, Fa, Qaf, Kaf, Lâm, Mîm, Nun, Ha, Was, Ya.—Pub.*

15

veins bringing the blood to your brain and your sudoriferous glands accelerating the production of sweat. Your little leather bag and your electronic bric-a-brac will not protect you. We will act in due time, if the Most Merciful, full of mercy, so deigns! Every move we make, every step we take, every human breath, every blade of grass—nothing exists outside His will. You should know that. So why must we remind you of the extent of His power?

We know who you are, and we will soon find out why you have returned. Meanwhile, let me tell you that I will personally follow your investigation with particular interest.

No sooner had you arrived than you gave away lots of money to redeem yourself, to smother your guilt or show what a great man you are. But you're still petty: your generosity goes just so far. With your balding head and your little intellectual's glasses, you're like a sand snake slithering this way and that. Maybe you want to keep acting like a big shot; well, you should know that I'm just a nobody. Nothing but a modest servant, just a bee on the scale of our Koranic values.

I am merely the scribe of our very pious and very venerable Master. I am the ember in the fire that flares up at the breath of his word. Apparently he and I have been sentenced to death. But you must know everything about our fate, isn't that right? We are incarcerated in a high security prison, totally isolated, on a desert island at the far end of the Gulf of Tadjoura. A tall lad with his lips tight shut slides a plate of rice under the door of our cell once a day. Click-clack! He is our only contact with the world.

We have been sentenced to death, they say. Who can send someone to the gallows and remain so ignorant of the fact that Allah the Almighty is the only Master? Who can deny that our life is in the hands of the Eternal? As for me, I am only the frail wrist of my venerable Master. I take down his dictation. I have lived next to him for so long that the words go from his holy mouth to my hand without a hitch. I am proud of serving him with constancy and passion.

My state of mind must be incomprehensible to you. You are not of this world. You are no longer of this world. We parted ways very early, by the grace of The All-Knowing. We do not consort with the same people; we do not live in the same cities. We do not breathe the same air. We are as antagonistic as day and night, you and me. You never should have set

●

foot here again. Now it is too late. You will drain your cup to the very dregs. For the moment, we have other tasks ahead of us, far more important than the small challenge of your return. We will carry them out with the aid of The Most Merciful, full of mercy.

They Call Me Djib!

NOTEBOOK 1. TUESDAY, 3 OCTOBER.

Yesterday at dawn I left the biggest hotel in the country and set out for the Gulf of Tadjoura, the cradle of maritime trafficking in everything under the sun. I was operating with a straw hat I'd bought on Place Menelik as my only disguise. Tossed about by the early morning swell in the unsafe little dhow, I looked just like a tourist stirred by nostalgia, rediscovering the charms of his country with tears in his eyes—a country he's not in touch with any more, except through Internet Explorer and Google Maps.

I have no desire to attract attention. I earned my spurs in a specific sector of the world of international business. I am part of that new elite with no permanent ties, at home everywhere, and foreign everywhere.

Today sovereign states are losing ground, becoming denationalized in the big picture of globalization. They see whole chunks of their sovereignty crumble away, given over to conglomerates. Trapped in the web of the information networks which make it obvious that they can no longer control bank data or the slogans of activist groups, states organize in their turn as they try to struggle out of this huge net.

I have been trained to disorganize these states and weaken them still more, so as to benefit multinational companies and their stockholders. It is lucrative work but it has its dangers. The straw hat and flowery shirt I bought from an Indian merchant on Place Menelik are my best camouflage.

I was reading *The Nation*, the country's only newspaper, on board the little sailboat. A government paper, of course. A two-day-old article minimized the firepower of the Islamist groups that control the backcountry. Out of habit, I was wearing an inexpressive mask on my face and did not flinch under the mocking remarks of the mechanic. He was an emaciated guy of no particular age, all gnarled muscles and more agile than a cat. I would never want to start a fight with him. First, one must know how to control oneself, keep one's analytic cool. Second, that would be professional misconduct. Third, he might beat the living daylight out of me, for I've been short of breath lately.

As I remained silent, he thought I didn't speak the languages of the country. Not one word came out of my mouth during the forty-two minutes that the crossing lasted. I kept reading and rereading the article dated Saturday, 30 September, to try to appear composed.

Suddenly everyone jumped out of the boat. The fishermen and people who live on the island have many jobs waiting for them throughout the day. The sailboat was leaving again in half an hour, just enough time to unload its merchandise and clean the deck with big buckets of water. I got back to Djibouti before nightfall, by the same sailboat that had made four round trips under a metallic-blue sky.

Oddly, on my way back the quarrelsome mechanic was not to be seen. He must have been sleeping off his khat in some port, or diving with tourists in search of underwater ecstasy. Besides a few useless snapshots, two or three sketches and a handful of fine sand, my harvest on Devil's Islets was zero. I had intended to have a close look at the condition of the roads, get a sense of the political situation in this district known for its resistance to the dictates of the capital, and gather some information about the high-security prison that comes up in every conversation.

And yet, right in front of these little islands where everything is all calm and sea breezes blow gently, a new page of history is being written. An ambiguous page that clashes with the austere beauty of these stony deserts. The two islets are commonly called Devil's Island, just like the famous island of the same name in French Guiana. That, too, was used as a penal colony, though on a smaller scale. A new adventure dawns for them now.

The local press eagerly related the origin of this 'extraordinary human adventure'. How many kilometres of warehouses were built, roads laid out, tunnels dug, dunes dynamited? How many tons of sand unearthed, of stones assembled, of cemeteries razed and families displaced? How many billions of dollars converted into Djibouti francs and then borrowed, invested or exchanged? How many arms worn out? How many zombies with broken bodies and minds teeming with illusions left for dead? No statistics. Polite silence.

Welcome to the new industrial park desired and designed by Dubai. The showpiece of the United Arab Emirates in the Horn of Africa. A haven of peace with a scent of salt. Projects, more projects, and still more projects. The country has caught this new fever. It even has a truly Pharaonic project: the construction of the longest bridge in the world. Yes, right here, in this corner of Africa which looks like the American Far West in miniature. Everything has been decided: the blueprint, the budget, the material and all the rest. We are told that the bridge will be built in less than two years for sure. It will rescue thousands of people from unemployment. It will flatter the bottomless pride of two heads of state. It will cross the Red Sea and connect Yemen and Djibouti, in other words Africa and Asia. Twenty-nine and a half kilometres long, it will see the light of day with the help of The Bountiful, without Whom nothing is possible! More prosaically, it will be the creation of the famous Middle East Development Corporation, the BTP Company of the Saudi Tarik Mohammed bin Laden. Its technical design and construction has already been given to Noor City Development, a firm of architects based in Silicon Valley. A new city called Madinat an-Noor or City of ight will arise. It will have a twin on the Yemenite side. More than Cleopatra's nose, this bridge will change the face of this region of the world.

Nothing more has filtered through since the press conference, which I'd watched through videoconference. Yet the splendour displayed at the presentation of the project dazed more than one foreign journalist specially shipped over by their offices in London, Paris, New York, Singapore, Doha and Abu Dhabi. Who will gain from this manna suddenly fallen from heaven? What about the thousands of millions that were spent just for this public relations operation?

Finding even the slightest clue is no easy task. Nobody trusts anything or anyone. They distrust me, the native turned foreigner—a native with no turban, and worse still, no beard. And yet all I had to do was follow the eyes of a shepherd I passed by on a hilltop or notice the nervousness of the porter—a child who looked like an old man—who picked up my suitcase on the steps of Ambouli airport, to feel the rage and frustration stewing inside each of them.

Denise, my French-Canadian girlfriend, had warned me: When you dip one foot into this land, you'll long to dive into it completely and drag other people with you. Welcome to the eye of the cyclone. The desert of silence. The paradise for nouveaux riche, *made in Dubai.*

Ever since the American armed forces have taken up residence here, the little Republic of Djibouti has benefited from a renewal of interest. France, its historical ally, no longer threatens to leave it to its sad fate—famine, war and oblivion. Nor to abandon it to its three starving, belligerent neighbours: Somalia, Ethiopia and Eritrea. France still sits enthroned in majesty, though it no longer inspires anyone. With dispatches, studies and missions, it continues to undermine the country while never failing to remind everyone of its boundless generosity. It sees the population as a bunch of beggars. Nothing but beggars, hooked on the local drug from noon to midnight.

And yet there is still a God for the wretched of the earth, Denise would say. The war against terror— now that's a miracle weapon. The *war-on-terror* chant picked up by all American editorialists from the *New York Times* to the *San Diego Union-Tribune*, quick to catch on to the new gospel of the White House, has changed the deal: the misery of some means the survival of the others. The new world order is a fine windfall for the people here. That doctrine is the backbone, the flow of blood simultaneously irrigating the Pentagon, Wall Street and K Street.

There's a little crew of them here, partying noisily, with big American flags on display. Swaggering around, badmouthing Afghans, Palestinians and Iraqis. Keeping the fallout from the financial bonanza for themselves, through cunning or violence.

But I have to admit that this new world order meant a new order for me, too. I was about to take a forced leave, fix up an old shack in the Gatineau Valley before going back to my position as part-time Assistant Lecturer in the IT Networks Laboratory at McGill University in Montreal in spring. And now here I am with a new contract, or more precisely a new mission, as we say in our jargon. War, as everyone knows, cannot wait. And it's not all bad. It's a stimulus to business and it strengthens the muscles of the stock market. As business never stops, neither do armed conflicts. There are always new markets to explore, new partners to consult, new logos to design, new directions to take and new masters to advise. I am a link in that chain of transnational command. A foot soldier of the shadows.

On my birth certificate my name is Djibril. People have called me Djib ever since I was a little child. *Call me Djib, that's it*! I announce in English. I must say it's very convenient in North America where you rub shoulders with people from the four corners of the earth who cooperate and trade so naturally, leaving behind anything that might prevent business from running smoothly. Unpronounceable patronymics and markers of identity are crushed, simplified and shortened. Elsewhere and yesterday forgotten. The past is dead, long live the future!

Call me Djib! I learned to do things the way they do. Short, smooth, efficient. No time for long historical and genealogical explanations. And yet here in this country, there is a legend that has pursued me since my birth. I would be called Djib, like this city and this country the colour of the sirocco. I was born on 26 June 1977, on the eve of Independence. I'm older by one day than the national flag they raised on 27 June, a little after midnight in an empty lot next to the Arhiba neighbourhood. A few seconds past midnight, my twin brother Djamal gave his first cry in the family courtyard, without the assistance of a midwife. As I was expelled twenty-eight minutes before my brother, still dazed, like a snail stuck in its slime, I was the first to salute the raised flag. I was healthy and cried loudly. Not my brother, who almost failed to let out his first cry. He still bears the marks of his difficult birth: a skull more elongated and a body punier than mine.

On the marshy ground where we once used to run breathlessly after a deflated soccer ball, they've now built the main soccer stadium of the country, a shopping mall, housing developments and even nice houses for expatriates. I remember that in first grade, in the schoolyard, there was a little group of us born on the same historic evening.

All that is very far away. I don't hear from my family any more, nor from my twin brother nicknamed 'Number 28' or more often '*Mister* 28' because he came into the world twenty-eight minutes after I did. I also used to call him 'Little Brother', because at that age, the birthright of the older one—even if older by half an hour—is sacred. All that is far, far away. The past is dead, long live the future. *Call me Djib*! In North America, I learned to be short, smooth and effective.

'*How you doing today, Sir?*'

'*Oh, thanks! My name is Djib! Call me Djib!*'

●

Ba

In the name of Allah the Most Merciful, full of mercy.
Praise be to Allah the Lord of Worlds. The Most Merciful, full of mercy, the Master of the Day of Judgement.

O you sand snake, learn that the Day of the Last Judgement is not yet at hand! By the grace of The Generous One, we have been blessed with a gentle day since dawn. A fine rain began to fall early on, offering us its freshness. Ah, how enviable is our little prison island, now that the water particles have reached the very depths of this isolated cell! Our fate is bearable in these vaporous moments where all is mystery and silence. Praise our Lord for His works in this world. We feel invigorated by this blessing that no novice in quest of The Most Lofty would have refused.

If you were one of our own, you apprentice investigator, I would have addressed a prayer to you, too, saying this: 'May this day be all you wish it to be. May the peace of The Majestic One rest in your thoughts, take control of your dreams from this moment on, and may all your fears be definitively vanquished. May God show Himself today in an exceptional way, a way you have never previously experienced. May your joyful desires be accomplished, your dreams fulfilled and your wishes granted. I pray for your faith to take on a new dimension. I pray for your territory to expand and I pray for you to take a great step towards your destiny in the ministry to which Prophet Muhammad called us. I pray for peace, health, happiness and the true imperishable love of The One.' That is what I would have said. But you need the right kind of ears to hear such a prayer!

Listen to this little story if you have a little time to devote to spiritual things. As for running after things that are virtual and artificial, I'm not worried about you: at that, you're a champion. But listen.

In days of old, men, animals, plants and all the creatures of Allah's earth lived peacefully together. One day, the owl got out of line. Remember how he spread the bad news over the whole surface of man's earth? He let the enemy know the hiding place of our Prophet Muhammad, may his name be praised forever! Ever since that day, the owl hangs around close to Satan.

You are of the same breed as that bird of ill omen. For only he who has lost his image and his language, he who has lost his markings and his shadow, only he recites Satanic verses and joins the company of the Devil. And he who suffers from temporary loss of memory has no other recourse than to recite the Hadith. All the terms defining God and all the suras will come to him if he opens wide his heart. Humbly, he must welcome them in his heart of hearts. And he will find the right, straight path again, if it pleases The Magnanimous! Amin.

·

Marines and Mirages

Like a mirage they appeared on the crest of the first dune. They were walking. I remember their gait as if it were yesterday. It was during our first family hike into the back country. Djamal and I were six years old.

They were walking. They could have been spotted from far off, ever since these nomads had crossed the great abyss at the foot of the Goda Mountains. Swathed in a veil of dust, they were walking, tumbling down the rocks of time. They had climbed the rocky plateau in stages, they had gone around the gulf. They were heading south now. The men were walking at the head of the caravan with the dromedaries on their heels. Then the boys, followed by the girls, the donkey, the sheep and the goats. The children who were too young brought up the rear of the caravan with the women. From time to time a hand would wipe away the sweat wrinkling a brow. A hand oblivious of hunger and thirst, for the moment. The goatskin

32

vessels fit into the backs of the women. The rifles were slung across the backs of the men. Two or three little boys of our age, naked to the waist, were running in front of the dromedaries' feet. Not for one moment did they stop. God knows what their goal was as they trudged along. They kept on walking, their silhouettes vanishing over the edge of the horizon. Nothing set them apart from us, sedentary people, except for a few details of dress. Except for that habit of staring into the distance or observing the flight of a condor. They were walking the way Grandpa Assod once walked; he, too, was born in a desert camp whose name nobody could remember.

Grandpa Assod had roamed the earth, the skies, and even the seas. Everywhere he had enjoyed the unlimited freedom he'd always wanted. He had been a horseman, a sailor, a soldier, a pilgrim five or six times, a cook for the French Navy, a guard in the penal colony of French Guiana—the most austere of them all, on Devil's Island, the exact same place where Captain Dreyfus had been detained for four long years. And, of course, a nomad like all our ancestors. But before he died, yes, before heaven became his last home, Grandpa Assod would still not trust the modern world and its accessories, like the telephone, the refrigerator or the television. His sons, city-dwellers to the tips of their toes, would not trust an object as ordinary as the telephone. They used it reluctantly, and only for emergencies.

'This machine bothers me, I can never see the face of the person who's talking to me,' he complained one day as he hung up our neighbours' phone. He hadn't noticed the three flies drowned at the bottom of the Fanta bottle next to the phone. We had. But Djamal and I always had a good eye for microscopic details. Our family wasn't rich enough to have a phone at the house—the shack would be closer to the truth. We had to cross the street to communicate something or, more rarely, to take a call.

'Grandpa, everything new is scary.' That's what we told him in chorus from the height of our twelve years put together. For once, he wasn't listening to us, to the great displeasure of 'Little Brother', much more irascible than I was.

At that time no adult paid any attention to us. Especially not our father. Grandfather and his eldest son, our father, were very different. Grandpa Assod was

tender and affectionate but Father was just like his
cousins, neighbours and friends with whom he recited
four out of the five daily prayers—the dawn prayer
taking place in our communal bedroom still plunged
in darkness. Why would he have paid any attention to
our comments and questions that tormented only our
poor childish souls? Why would he have been any
different from the other fathers? No reason for it.
Hadn't he drunk the same bittersweet milk as the men
of his clan? Hadn't he worn the same tuft of hair before
his adolescence? At the same age as us hadn't he run
after the same young camels, singing the little songs
that shepherd boys sing? Hadn't he married a distant
cousin he had never seen before, whose name had been
whispered to him a few weeks before the wedding by
the matronly women he affectionately called 'aunts'
and who were not his real aunts but simply his mother's
cousins or, more precisely, women of his mother's
clan? Didn't he think that the earth was as flat as a pile
of cow dung?

And yet we had such a longing for a very different, very accessible, very close father that we could
have felt his breath caressing the nape of our necks.
Why should we have enjoyed this privilege? What did

my twin brother and I have over the other children of the neighbourhood to give us the right to demand more attention, warmth and affection?

'Father!' The cry of a frustrated 'Little Brother' would ring through the thin walls and rise to heaven. I imitated him immediately: 'Father!'

'A curse on your father!' our mother would answer. Or was it another voice emerging from the night?

Coming into the world into a family like that was no easy business.

I'm almost thirty now. I've changed a lot. Here, too, everything has changed drastically and yet nothing has really changed. You have to think twice to get a sense of it. The country is being transformed under our bewildered eyes. Our eyes impatient to see something like the fulfilment of a prediction. You can see it in those new construction sites that have popped up like mushrooms. You can see it in the extension of the capital, caught in expansion fever under the impetus of the Unted Arab Emirates. Due to its geographical position and stability, my little country has charmed the high strategists of the Pentagon and the businessmen of the

Persian Gulf, Dubai first and foremost. It's a logical union, as they have common interests.

What the best-informed media used to call a pure hypothesis has become a reality. After first occupying a base right next to Ambouli airport, in the summer of 2002 the Americans set up the command centre of the Combined Joint Task Force for the Horn of Africa in a camp abandoned by the French Army. According to the words of a Pentagon directive, the goal of this new base is 'to spot, contain and finally neutralize the transnational terrorist groups operating in the region. To take the ground out from under the feet of those evil entities looking for safe havens, isolated islets, outside support and logistical assistance.'

American forces feel safe only inside this camp rented from the Djiboutian government for the modest sum of thirty-two million dollars a year. Camp Lemonier is a fortified base, protected by a double surrounding wall bristling with watchtowers, infrared cameras and concrete barriers, as well as several rows of barbed wire. Heavily armed, helmeted Marines in body armour stand guard twenty-four hours a day. In this hostile environment where bad memories can be stirred up and old wounds reopened, they don't play around with the GIs' safety. Yet the new Rome is not afraid of anything. Quite the opposite: it has unhesitatingly charged ahead. 'No corner of the world is too far off, no mountain too high, no cave or bunker too deep to put our enemies beyond our reach,' trumpeted the Secretary of Defence just last week in the bi-monthly *Foreign Affairs*, considered to be the bible of diplomacy.

The road connecting the camp to the capital stretches out in a long ribbon of asphalt. Dried out by the khamsin and worn down by traffic, from noon to three in the afternoon it produces the best mirages in the area. Under the delighted eyes of the radio-activity experts the road goes from liquid to gas and back to liquid before returning to solid at the end of the afternoon. It is precisely this crucial section of road that was hit by the first type 101 home-made bomb a few days ago. No victims, little damage. It seems to be a warning at no cost to anyone.

In other times, the thirteenth half-brigade of the Foreign Legion and the infantrymen of the fifth Joint Overseas Regiment played their roles openly, less harshly, in a more relaxed way. There, too, things have changed. Unlike the French, the two thousand

American soldiers live in isolation, in aseptic, air-conditioned autarchy. They never set foot outside the base. They are strictly forbidden to go out unless they're in a heavily armed group, in unmarked white Toyota SUVs. To go out on security patrols or lead information campaigns against AIDS they use Humvees with a machine gun mounted on top.

As I went over the data sheet on the base, I couldn't help noticing that the equipment of the Americans is the same as in Iraq, even though the nature of their missions is very different, at least officially. I really wonder what my twin brother has deduced from this, rebel that he is—or, more precisely, as he was. Perhaps Djamal has changed, like this country and like me. Who knows? I haven't seen him for fifteen years.

The mission orders of the Joint Force are as long as the list of medical prescriptions for a patient in critical condition. In Washington and elsewhere, the region is thought to be the greatest powder keg in the world after Afghanistan and Iraq. Troops and movements of every kind and persuasion have been reported there. Several local intelligence agencies are murmuring that a students, of a new kind, well versed in the cognitive sciences, are pouring in from distant lands—Sudan, Gaza, Nigeria, Peshawar or Kurdistan—to train in al-Qaedaesque fortified camps. Not to mention that the stinging defeat of those same American forces in the battle of Mogadishu is still in everyone's memory. The urban guerilla of the Somali warlord Mohamed Farrah Aïdid had wounded the morale of the best-equipped and trained army in the world. The fact that Aïdid's troops were secretly trained and armed by instructors from the international movement al-Qaeda al-Jihad, founded in 1987 by Osama Bin Laden and more commonly called al-Qaeda, takes nothing away from that whipping. It happened on 3 October 1993. Hollywood made a Manichaean film out of it: *Black Hawk Down* and, lately, a video game.

In the eye of the cyclone, I'm trying to keep cool, to remain calm and methodical. Yet all these changes are giving me a vague feeling of unease, a furtive discomfort. As my investigation progresses I can't help noticing minute jolts to my body.

It all began with a banal headache. Then there was a stiffness in my neck that settled in little by little.

At certain moments now I can't breathe. At first I put it all down to jet lag or not being used to the heat any more. In time it will go away, I told myself encouragingly. And now my little childhood voice has come back to me. It had not yet found its way to my throat before this return to my native country, but now here it is, intact. My Canadian colleagues wouldn't have recognized its timbre and those sharp intonations. It reaches my ears very distinctly now, rounding up a whole flock of memories that spring from the past. It brings back to the surface a self I hadn't known existed. True, a self too little for my adult body, but a perfectly recognizable self.

With this voice, I have come full circle. I am the alpha and the omega, the beginning and the end. It brings back a whole string of impressions, like that sandy beach I hadn't seen for years. That's where I would come to sit and listen to the waltz of the waves and the song of the gulls with 'Little Brother' and my grandfather Assod, who was never very far away.

Everything has changed and nothing has changed over the last twenty-two years. The beach is deserted. There is more garbage, more cardboard boxes and more plastic bottles. Even today I can't quite manage to feel completely alone here. Everything seems deserted but that is far from the truth. Opening my eyes wide is all it takes to pierce the veil of this illusion. There's an old man over there. Bony and forlorn. He is sitting with his hands flat on his knees and his head bent. He is contemplating a ballet of ants. He floats among the creatures that haunt his mind.

Financed by the powerful Dubai Ports World, the third port complex of the country is emerging from the rubble of the little village of Doraleh, eight kilometres away from the capital. It looms up before our eyes.

●

Ta

O miscreant of Montreal, you must know nothing of our daily rituals! Do you know that Muslims, wherever they may arrive in this vast world, have to face Mecca to perform their prayers? The Kaaba is the direction in which they aim. If this condition is not met the prayer will be worthless. Thus one must always verify the direction of Mecca or the *qibla*. There was a time when the faithful got along by looking at the stars. Then the compass was discovered, which reassured many believers. But all too often some half-believers trust their instincts and pray towards the rising sun, without realizing that the geographical position of France or Canada, for instance, is not the same for the countries of the Maghreb or the Middle East. One must then explain to them why they are in error, which is not easy when they are as pigheaded as you are.

Do you know that the country you live in was the site of highly scientific debates to determine the calculation of the *qibla*? You're not going to join the rank of the true believers any time soon but I'll give you the formula anyway, for there really is one. All you have to do is determine the latitude and longitude of the place of prayer, that is, the coordinates of the point where you happen to be on the terrestrial globe. That direction is given in relation to geographic north. You can use a compass, it's more convenient. You should know, however, that the compass points to the magnetic north, which is slightly off geographic north. Finally, you should know that the latitude of the holy city of Mecca is 21° 26′ N and its longitude is 39° 49′ E, while the latitude of the North Pole is 90°. I'll spare you the rest of the calculation. It is high time for you to return to a place of prayer. There is still time to return to the bosom of Allah.

The Unbelievers

My new notebook is empty or almost empty, except for a few geothermic considerations. I should be more active. More incisive. There's not a moment to lose if I want to hand in my report as quickly as possible. And yet I'm navigating in the fog. Worse, I remain in a state of inertia. My little childhood voice is taking me down a slippery slope where elsewhere and yesterday are all mingled. I am indecisive and fearful. I'm afraid of opening old wounds. I am well aware that even greater pain and setbacks await me round the corner of every little street of my childhood.

My little voice from long ago is quivering with impatience and can't wait to come out. It is flooding me now, I can feel it resonating inside me and suddenly it is covered by the hoarse smoker's voice of my grandfather Assod tumbling down the rocks of time. Now I'm transported to the maternal family of my grandfather. A family settled by the Bay of Zeïlah for several generations. Zeïlah? A city full of history and misunderstandings; my grandfather told me about it often.

The mysteries of a white man tortured and nailed to his cross, blood gushing out of him, more dead than alive, had not stirred the multitudes in the region of Zeïlah. At least that's what our indefatigable grandfather used to tell us. Our ancestors did not look kindly on the perspective of getting crucified here below for an uncertain happiness in the beyond, he said. To the Christian paradise they preferred the connection to sand and wind, the wedding of earth and water and the songs and dances of the volcano. He insisted that surely, a long time after their bodies take their leave, the spirits of the ancestors live as nomads in the region, from Jigjiga to Kabah Kabah, from Yoboki to Awdal and further, on the vast land of men. Their spirits will walk along with the clan, with other human beings, with the earth and its thousand animals to hunt, praise or tame. They will always be in this world, they will enjoy every moment, from the first signs of dawn to the endless evening of eternity. The spirit will always be alive. Its other name is the dust from which we come and to which we shall return.

But our ancestors, Grandpa Assod would insist between two fits of coughing, couldn't conceive of possessing land, of claiming it for one's own, of cutting it up; parcelling it out or planting a flag on it was foreign to their ways. We do not possess land but honour it, live on it decently and celebrate it by going about our daily chores: leading the cattle to graze, milking the camels, welcoming the traveller on the roads, tapping the palm wine when there is some. Cultivating our little plot of millet if we happen to live on the generous hills of Hawd, he added for us, as we had never heard of that part of the country; keeping an eye on the way the streams are flowing, tending the bee hives and the sacred wood of the ancestors. Taking part in verbal jousts. Busily trading in goods and the exchange of nubile girls.

It is said that somewhere around Zeïlah, on that shore encased in fogs and dreams, there was even a permanent structure from which an infernal noise rang out periodically. It came from a huge metallic pitcher called bell. Children would be assembled there and sit in rows all day long to learn things they had to decipher from a piece of paper. Two men with skin and beards the colour of seashell kept them at a

47

respectful distance with nothing more than a stick. It was truly surprising that no clan had yet risen to confront them. Who could be sure these bearded stick-wielders walking at a turtle's pace were not scouts and road-openers for other, more ferocious, bearded men? It was said they were so transparent because they probably washed their bodies with asses' milk. They also dyed their white hair, hair they wore longer than that of our girls with erectile breasts, said Grandpa Assod.

And life went on, from moon to moon, from pasture to pasture. And one fine day the advent of a new messiah was announced, a man from Arabia who called himself holy, that is, sent by the one and only God. Hardly had he arrived than he began to range through the country in all directions, from the sea to the mountain and from desert to desert to preach again and again. And he delivered sermons to the shepherds who would not stop to greedily drink in his words. Of those he would say: They are innocent lambs who sin through ignorance and not through vice. And he tried to bring them back to the right path through threats and blackmail. Meanwhile, the moon kept on its course; the grass grew as soon as the rain ended and the cows calved. Milk foamed in the goatskins and no one knew what to do with the surplus. A creamy white halo covered up the burial mounds and anthills where the souls of our ancestors rest.

Strange as it seems, my grandfather Assod's voice often blots out the voices of my departed parents. While the memories of my grandfather surface easily, memories of my parents remain a blur. I don't know if it's the same for my twin brother. What memory has Djamal retained of our childhood?

●

Tha

In the name of Allah the Most Merciful, full of mercy.
Praise be to Allah the Lord of Worlds. The Most Merciful, full of mercy, the Master of the Day of Judgement. It is Allah we worship, Allah we implore. Allah,
who leads us on the path of righteousness, the path
of those on whom Allah lavishes His blessings, not of
those who anger Allah or those who stray from His
path. Our fate is in His hands for all eternity.

A revenant cannot be killed, says one of our old
proverbs. Patience, you will be dealt with. Nothing is
urgent for he who desires the Eternal Kingdom. I am
going to tell you a little detail about my venerable
Master. One of those little signs that cut through the
layers of time and give its author the reverberating
quality of myth. I'm also counting on your great
capacity of invention. In this prison, my venerable
Master prays sitting down. His legs can no longer bear
the weight of his body. His knees were broken by the
torturers but his devotion is intact. Often the time

devoted to our prayers flows by peacefully, opening on to long introspections. One prayer calls forth another and I join him in spirit. Now we are prostrate side by side with our beads in our hands. Now we are at the doorstep of the dwelling of the Lord. Lord, You are the most merciful and the most compassionate. Welcome us into the sanctuary where You reside, grant us permission to enter into the serenity of Your dwelling. Amin!

The Angel of History

My heart is already pitching towards Montreal and it's only Wednesday noon. It was in Montreal that I emerged from my chrysalis: there I became the man I am now. In that metropolis I found everything that makes up the everyday fare of an enviable life: an angelic woman, a job, a roof, friends. I feel as if I were born in Montreal, as if the first eighteen years spent with my family and my twin brother (who is invisible today) didn't count at all.

As a child I dreamed of being an only son so as to get all of my mother's attention. To no avail. I saw my childhood and adolescence go by at lightning speed without getting an ounce of the affection I longed for. Many times people in the family—but not my mother—told me I was sensitive, irritable and unpredictable. But also humble, ambitious, unloved and instinctive and creative, too. As an adult, I can be humble, clever, full of complexes, or not loving enough. And the veil that hid the origin of my violent, compulsive urges, first against my brother and then against myself, is slowly lifting. In Montreal I learned to put up with myself, to like myself, if possible, in order to sleep peacefully inside my skin. It is only at this price that I can move forward in life. Live life to the fullest. Love others.

For a long time I dreamed I had no mother. In reality, it's as if I had lost her when I was very young. I hardly knew her. I was raised by a strict grandmother who inculcated in us the few rules I have assimilated. I have forgotten everything about my mother, as if she had no face. She had forgotten me first when she set her heart on my twin brother, giving all her attention only to him, showering kisses only on him. In moments of high anxiety, I used to tell myself it was my mother who separated me from my brother early on. She's the one who turned him into my enemy, I would say to myself bitterly before coming back to my senses.

No concrete memory connects me to my mother. Not one story, caress, slap or hug. I have a hungry vacuum in the hollow of my chest that only the warmth of a maternal body against mine could fill. That was the time when I decided to provoke my brother and defy my father before breaking out of the family web. To follow my own path, alone, no matter what. The only sweet memory of my childhood: my encounter with a stranger—an orphan named David. I think we liked each other a lot, he and I. We rapidly became very close. Together we admired the junk dealers on Place Arthur-Rimbaud. We were insepa-rable. We often met on Siesta Beach. We used to run after the fish that were bold enough to swim near the beach, especially the skates.

Years later, I earned my pocket money by assist-ing the projectionist of the Odeon Cinema, in the heart of the European part of the city. I was already interested in the media, unlike my brother, who spent his time devouring books. When I went out into the fresh air he would lounge about in the half-light of our room with a book near at hand.

At that time the French infantry and naval bases were in full swing. The draftees were regular cus-tomers of the movies and the many bars. They weren't men but human packs who stormed the two rooms of our cinema, the most imposing of the capi-tal. Some discontented spirits from Algeria wanted to baptize it Lagardeville, after the first governor of that territory, Viscount Léonce Lagarde de Rouffey-roux, and also rename the Olympia Cinema, our main competitor, in the same way.

For a while that's where I found a true family. Warm. Carefree and joyful. That's where I lived through my first exile—an exile that was French in every way. On the thin skin of my memories, I've kept a few caresses from that exile. You might think soothing people's pain and treating them is a nurse's job but, believe it or not, that's exactly what I did as a projectionist. I used images to treat all those young men torn away from their farms or housing projects and thrown under the vertical sun of Djibouti. I loved that job and its small pleasures. I loved the moments before the screening, like the twilight which gives minarets their imposing silhouette. I loved the call to evening prayer that would rise from the nearby mosque. I loved everything about those transitory moments when the city shook itself off after the long lethargy of the afternoon. The horns of taxis and the clamour of street vendors filling the streets. And the seedy crowds of the night mixing together till dawn. No more rank, no more hierarchy. Just animal warmth, the pulsation of the night, the gleam of smiles. Just men and women glued to the bars, busy eating and drinking, or laughing, sprawled out under the pergolas. I loved nightlife there. I would even tolerate the senseless howling of the legionnaires. I'd take a shower before putting on my legendary outfit: lagoon blue Bermuda shorts, light sandals and flowery shirt open to the solar plexus. This was my uniform. My diver's suit for plunging into the night and seeking out its spicy amber. I would have a little twinge of anxiety every time I opened the projection booth door at 6.40 p.m. Gripped by a mixture of apprehension and exultation when the first reel began and the wall became covered not with the first images of the film but with the pictures of the newsreels and commercials that had arrived from Paris the previous week. That excitement remained as strong as it had been on the first day. The cinema filled up quickly, ready for a new evening of adventure and dreams.

All that is so far away. But the sight of that cinema is enough to bring up the fragrance of the past up to the surface.

My investigation is progressing very slowly. I'm stumbling over many obstacles. I'm waiting for the turning point. It's always like that when I'm on the job. To be honest, I had some doubts from the very beginning. I thought of giving up a number of times. I hadn't reckoned with Denise: she got me back in the saddle every time, explaining that I was going through a stretch of desert which felt like a waste of time, but no, it wasn't a waste of time, not at all. I was unconsciously gathering a bundle of impressions and sensations—and thus, precious information.

Denise had only half convinced me. So why on earth did I leave the satin skies of Montreal? Did I really have to return to the land of my childhood? They say that the only true mysteries are the ones we invent for ourselves. That we take great pains to confuse nightmares and reality. I studied science— chemistry and physics—in order to stop dreaming— contrary to my brother who loved literature. Physics for its precision. Chemistry for its perpetual invention and magical finds. Not forgetting maths as a foundation. I needed powerful rails and a steady base so that life would cease to be something that merely floated around me.

I studied all that in Montreal. That city saved my life; I would have gone astray, just drifting aimlessly along. Rubbing shoulders with shady people, doing just about anything to escape a pointless life. Montreal gave a meaning to my existence and, more prosaically, a doctorate in computer science. Montreal had a face when I met it for the first time. An oval face, with sky-blue eyes. Pearly skin. A turtleneck sweater. That was Denise, sitting on a bench in the garden of the centre for foreign students in Paris, the Cité Internationale on Boulevard Jourdan.

I had been dragging myself around feeling miserable for weeks and months. I shot out calls to everyone like signals from a beacon. Denise was the only one who smiled at me. And it was love at first sight. Despite her Quebecois accent, Denise was born in Paris in 1968. She is nine years older than I am. Her father, Isaac Rosenzweig, an Austrian from Vienna, had enlisted in the Foreign Legion and was wounded in North Africa in 1961. I have no idea if he'd knocked around my native land, which was then called Côte Française des Somalis, or French Somaliland. A year later he married a fiery woman, half Norman, half Panamanian, a native of Trouville:

Elvira Triboulet. He became a waiter in a cafe; she became an actress and a stripper. They lived with their daughter in a sordid little hotel on Boulevard Ornano in the 18th arrondissement. The Rosenzweig family emigrated to Quebec right in the middle of the Velvet Revolution. They adopted Quebec and never left it except for excursions to Paris in winter. That's how Denise knows every little street, every neighbourhood, every piece of its history.

It was also in Paris, on another bench of the Cité Internationale, that Denise talked to me about another great walker in the City of Light. A philosopher of the past century: Walter Benjamin. She religiously kept his photo by Gisèle Freund tucked in her wallet, between Metro tickets and her coupons to the student cafeteria where we had our meals. It was Denise who introduced me to the secret life of this Walter Benjamin. Luckily, I was won over, not right away but much later. By his encyclopedic mind, his intuitive method and, above all, by his conception of history, which was not theoretical or arid in the least. It appealed to me because it seemed as sensitive to human beings as the stories my Grandpa Assod used to tell. I, too, have adopted the 'angel of history' and made it mine. Here is its description, as the German Jewish philosopher restores it for us:

There is a painting by Paul Klee called Angelus Novus. *It shows an angel who seems about to move away from something he is staring at. His eyes are wide open, his mouth is agape, his wings are spread. This is how the Angel of History must look. His face is turned toward the past. Where we perceive a chain of events he sees a single catastrophe which keeps piling wreckage upon wreckage and hurls it at his feet. The angel would like to stay, wake the dead, and make whole what has been shattered. But a storm is blowing in from Paradise; it has got caught in his wings with such violence that the angel can no longer close them. This storm drives him irresistibly into the future, to which his back is turned, while the pile of debris before him grows skyward. This storm is what we call progress.*

I am sure Grandpa Assod would have appreciated this fable. As for me, I began to identify with Klee's angel.

●

Jim

By the grace of the Magnificent, I am pleased to record the sermons, parables and commentaries of my venerable Master. All that issues from his marvellous mouth is lassoed by my pen and fixed on paper. This knowledge will be transmitted to future generations by a whole line of reciters who will be as reliable as they are scrupulous.

O you, playboy of the modern world, listen to this:

All cities look alike, but each has its own history and personality, says my venerable Master. To illustrate his adage, he takes the twelve cities of our region as examples: the city of Obock is desolate and amnesiac. Zeïlah, celebrated by Ibn Batuta as early as the fourteenth century, has remained ghostly, always looking back to its radiant past, when it was an outpost of the Ottoman Empire. Harar is sad to have lost its wanderer who went by the name of Arthur Rimbaud, and ended up embracing our faith. Mocha the Yemeni is inconsolable, unaware that its precious coffee became famous under other skies. The port of Assab looks greedily at the opposite bank of the Red Sea. Further to the north, Alexandria mopes dejectedly, dreaming of a rapid rebirth while waiting for the call of The Most Holy.

Having gone through the first six cities, my venerable Master has no intention of stopping when he's doing so well. He tells his beads as he catches his breath.

The city of Massawa, he continues, should fight to regain its place in our Umma, 'the best community ever raised for mankind' (Koran III:110). The harbour of Aden shows us its moonlike face, all huddled up on itself. The last brewery in the Persian Gulf was shut down almost three decades ago—thanks to us, he pronounces calmly. Closer to home, Tadjoura, with its seven legendary mosques, prays to heaven and waits for the manna of Allah while watching the big cargo ships that dock on the other bank. Berbera, once a Soviet military base, will regain the smile and importance worthy of its rank. Mogadishu, which only yesterday was torn by anarchy, stood up on its prayer carpet and has lived in peace and harmony ever since we transformed all its discos into places of prayer and contemplation. In this part of Somalia, once infested with pirates who feared neither God nor man, people now pray and curse the heathen— for example, that former Somali-Dutch deputy who's praised to the sky in the most conservative circles in America. That woman, known for her lies and her attacks on our religion, no longer goes anywhere without a bodyguard. Her days are numbered, for our forces are relentless.

And you, the apprentice investigator, I want to tell you that you will be struck down by the same lightning. My venerable Master went further: Thank God, we do not lack armed recruits. At prayer-time, our mosque-schools are full to bursting. Here and elsewhere, people have finally understood that man does not live on earth only to produce goods, to buy and to seek pleasure. On no account can one miss the noonday prayer, *salât al dhor*.

At this time, of the twelve cities of the land, only Djibouti seeks out the infidels and offers herself to tourists. She shuns the green standard of our Prophet—may His Name be praised both day and night! She wanders around in her own night: the interminable winter of *Jahiliyyah*. Djibouti and her backcountry are consumed by fire but they do not know it yet. Together, they will drain their cup to the dregs.

Seven months ago only a madman would have bet a dirham on this land, our venerable Master continues. The twelve cities were in the throes of endless agony and gripped by unshakable langour. They could feel the black bile of asthenia flowing deep inside their guts. Believe me, my child, they were paying the price of their estrangement, of their self-negation, of their unprecedented sins. Cradles of a fervour that was once authentic, they had thrown themselves into trade, body and soul. It was not easy to keep their faith, blessed a dozen times over. They descended, step by step, into that dark region where closeness to God is no longer the obsession of every moment, the ambition of a lifetime. For a long time they were proud of their ignorance, their recent wealth, their Western veneer. Forgetful of the poverty ravaging the backcountry, they cultivated flashy, ephemeral things. And the source of their faith dried up like the Sagallo wadi. They lost their bearings and fell back into childhood. They lost the sense of belonging to our civilization, which conquered the world and brought everywhere the two scales of justice, the teachings of the Koran and the coolness of our oases.

Why did it please these cities to disdain the beneficial effects of our faith which are praised the world over, from the Philippines to the dry, ardent lands of Spain?

Silence. I was unable to find an answer to the question of our venerable Master! I stopped asking him questions so as not to lose one crumb of his teaching. I am writing under his dictation, on old bits of paper that the wind has blown into our cell. It is not unusual that little rolls of paper reach us even here, in this high security prison. Who can stop the wind? We must thank God for the few pieces of paper that have reached us here just in the last five days. Thank God, the colossus with sealed lips who brings us our only bowl of white rice seems to pay no attention to the tricks of the wind.

•

Siesta Beach

My first excursion into the south of the country yielded nothing, just like the boat trip in the Gulf of Tadjoura. I might have known. The situation on the ground is tense. Dangerous as water speeding up as it nears the falls. The foreign media are throwing oil on the fire, playing on the nerves of the population. False news, rumours, manipulations. And while there hasn't been any loss of life yet, fear reigns triumphant. People hole up in their houses fearing other bombs, more murderous this time around. From human bombs to quality-assured projectiles, the palette is unlimited. Martyrs are legion in the slums. And yet three armed forces—the national army backed by the Marines and French overseas troops, which makes over twelve thousand well-equipped men—criss-cross the length and breadth of the territory, and the three land borders have been closed for a long time.

I still have two and a half days left. This afternoon, I visited the local authorities to get back my Canadian passport, which I had to give to the border police when I arrived a week ago. Administrative rules resemble the rules of chance more often than you'd think. But this time it all ended well. I put my stamped passport away in the safe of my hotel room. As for the rest, I'm holding my course. I have to keep on looking and thinking. Seeking advice from the spirit of ancestors like Grandpa Assod. Travelling to every corner of the country and going through every Koranic school, every mosque, even the smallest little town, with a fine-toothed comb. It is only at this price that luck will smile on me in the end.

Denise tells me that everything's fine in Montreal and she's rereading *A Berlin Childhood* by Walter Benjamin. As for me, I still haven't had the time to open my copy. And yet it's lying right on my bedside table.

Word of my return to the country has been going around. I had to put up with some new visits. Some of them official. Others, the most numerous, unexpected. And, of course, still not the slightest trace of

'Little Brother'. Everything gets around very quickly here, for everyone knows everyone else. And yet I'm staying on my guard. I follow my schedule to the letter, hour by hour. One of my childhood friends (are they still my friends? what do we have in common except for far-off, stale memories?) called me a traitor. I had noticed in particular that his cell phone rang like the azan, the call of the muezzin. Another, more generous, more educated as well, compared me to the golem, that clay creature molded by Rabbi Judah Löwi of Prague which comes back to haunt the city every thirty-three years.

I left a very long time ago; I am a man from elsewhere wearing a mask from here, with only borrowed memories in stock. I am a ghost trying to pierce the hardened crust of everyday life through dreams and imagination. Who trusts no one. Who arouses distrust and cannot even imagine the mountain of rumours piling up about him. When my research is over I will fly away, with no regret and no remorse. I will take along my notes and secrets for a transnational company domiciled in North America like me. Mission accomplished. I'll fly away to see Denise again and devour with her the autobiographical

writings of our favourite author. Goodbye Djibouti.
The rest is beyond my field of expertise. I have not
come here to change the world. My shoulders aren't
broad enough for that. To each his own little job.
Goodbye Balbala, Obock and Tadjoura! Hello Montreal, Quebec and Trois-Rivières!

We would often go sit on the deserted beach I'm
watching from my hotel window. La Siesta, that's its
name. At least it hasn't changed names. No need for
a Geographical Survey map to find it. I can see it from
my room. Here I am, with my little camcorder, film-
ing my childhood beach. I always felt the urge to lift
a corner of the veil, to examine the other side of the
set, not out of provocation but because shadow
reveals light, silence reveals words, an instant reveals
history. I am alone with my little voice, unwinding a
reel of the film of my past.

I can see us side by side, David and me. We used
to run from the Hamoudi mosque shoulder to shoulder, stride across the railroad tracks, charge onto the
beach and jump into the water at the same time. We
would swim a little, and then come out of the water as
one. Both of us were completely carefree. That was

the invisible wire that bound our two little bodies together as the swallow's saliva holds together the twigs that make up its nest. I was a year older but you were certainly the braver one. The most mischievous, too. I'm not saying that to make you look good, or because you're no longer here to contradict me, David—but because it's the truth. You had taken the place of my twin brother.

After all these years, nothing interests me more than the truth. Facts, dates. The truth and nothing but the truth. Using my zoom lens, I try to record the sand, the mud and the rocks of the beach; they, too, haven't changed or lied. If I must be faithful to something, it might as well be to that past. Besides, my long absence has cured me of the urge to run after mirages. Vanity is for young men on the make who want to conquer the world. Boasting is for small-time actors who buttonhole people and force them to listen.

We used to walk to Siesta Beach to listen to the whistle of the wind and the song of the gulls. We would stand in front of the sea in frightened, mute admiration. We would squeeze our fists tight enough to break our finger bones. Sometimes we would run after a skate that had ventured near the beach. But most often we'd be calm, motionless, like a squirrel that regains its balance with the plume of its tail. We sought out mysteries, like the path of birds in the sky. We were ready to sing for the waves which were once elevated to the rank of near-divinities.

David, at your age—at our age—you could not have suspected that people here have feared the sea since the dawn of time; they turn their back on it. The beach marks the final boundary of their movements. And that's something they don't like very much. But we both loved the beach like a first love. Two adolescents: two chance twins. Ever since the sixth grade, we promised each other we would never separate, come what may. Together we were one.

We had met a year earlier in the schoolyard of the Boulaos elementary school. Life lay before us. The sweet undulation of silence filled us with happiness. We loved the gentle north wind, which carries the monsoon and makes the acacias, reeds and prickly shrubs dance. We loved the south wind, heavy with dust, which gives the impression that the universe is honey-coloured, that fate isn't necessarily grim. Yes, we loved all that, and today I still love the boundless silence of this spot, for two worlds brush against each other and watch each other on this beach, even when nothing seems to be happening there. Two worlds that confront each other and tear each other apart before they find a semblance of balance. One world forever longed for, and another forever lost.

The fire of origins surges from the depths of this cove. Very few people ventured out here. From time to time a cart pulled by a donkey and loaded with dried seaweed would pass before us. Paddy boats, dhows and other sailboats went far out and returned. A crippled old man waiting only for death would stick his pilgrim's staff into the mud, soliloquizing with the pink flamingoes. With his net on his shoulder, an Arab fisherman would be dancing on the edge of the horizon. We'd give them a little wave. We would wait till they went off and wandered away into the mineral nakedness. It was precisely at those moments that you would take out your ballpoint pen and your rolled-up piece of paper from the pocket of your shorts. The features of your face would change. You had a cannibal look about you, overflowing with appetite and vitality. A voice light as the ocean breeze would immediately whisper to you: 'Write, boy, write! Pour your batch of words onto the paper! Write, because you, at least, never gave up trying to understand the world.' And the words would come out by themselves as if dictated by a voice from somewhere else, ready to be set down on paper. Four or five lines, depending on the day. Hardly more. You would read me what had come out of your pen, your hand, or rather your brain. You used to murmur, moving your lips as children do when they play out every character in the story they're telling, one after the other. You would read and reread a few times until you knew every word by heart. Then, satisfied, you nodded your head to reassure yourself. I would watch your little game in silence.

You would roll up the sheet of paper in a piece of plastic. To find it all you had to do was bend and pick it up off the ground. Which you did like an automaton, absorbed as you were in reading and reciting. There were pieces of plastic in all colours flying around all over the beach and hanging on the gorse bushes, cactus and wild shrubs. But you, David, you did not get distracted by the bits of plastic dancing in the wind. You carefully tied up the paper containing your thought of the day in a bit of plastic no wider than the palm of your hand. Then you would slip the whole thing in a plastic bottle and throw it into the sea. You did this at least once a week. More than a game, it had become an unchanging ritual. A bet with destiny, which was pulling the strings in the dark.

The gold of an untold secret never turns to ashes, you would tell me later, before our ways parted. So I was to keep this secret all my life. As teenagers, we distrusted the people around us. We kept quiet before those who thought they could sniff out our secret in no time, those who were able to read intent in the eye before the tongue gives it away. That's why we kept to ourselves, solitary as those two little islands in the middle of the sea.

When you weren't throwing messages into the Gulf, David, you were picking up other messages, do you remember? They regularly washed up on the beach. They were meant for you alone. You think I'm just rambling and embellishing everything? I don't have an ounce of imagination. I have no gift for invention. All my life, I have only written data sheets and lab reports. Brief, precise reports, readily comprehensible, like the one I'm supposed to hand over in a few days.

Those messages always began in the same way. The black ink and the paper were always the same. It was easy to imagine that the same person was behind those missives. Invariably the author used the same opening sentence. A ritual formula composed of two words: 'Dear Unknown'. The closing formula was just as laconic, containing three highly enigmatic words: '*In Libro Veritas*'.

For David, every missive he picked up was a source of infinite joy, and it rubbed off on me. Each word was put in, weighed and addressed only to him. And if I didn't grasp the overall plot at first, I succeeded, after a thousand hypotheses, in decoding fragments of the story of the man or woman who was sending these strange letters. By reading and rereading the letters—so ancient they looked as if they had been traced in the light of a tallow candle— by chewing on those words and enigmatic formulas over and over again, I succeeded in leaving the present and its perimeter of certainties. In opening myself up to the story and guessing the profile of its author and sensing the texture of his life and times.

Yes, even at our age we could suspect, David and I, that the life of this person had not been easy. Was he still in the land of the living? Was he simply dead? We imagined him as a kind of hermit with a little smile, bowed under the weight of years. He had to be an old man riddled with rheumatism, covered with the scars he had got from the penal colony, more dead than alive. Wondering about the life of this man—but who said it was a man!—was like stirring up the stuff that dreams are made on, the way a filmgoer standing in front of the closed door of a theatre can hear the music and bits of dialogue without ever being able to see a single image of the film.

We could imagine an old man born of the waves, the only fellow on Devil's Islets. A forlorn, wizened old man, his skin and clothes worn out by life. His destiny had to be measured by milestones, great historical facts. That's what you suspected, David. Our imagination danced over the moors of books and legends.

I left my hotel room with a ravaged heart and resumed my investigation with difficulty. The archives I consulted from afar, through professional channels or with Denise's help, all reach the same conclusion. Besides, the fact sheet established by the CIA (also available on *Wikipedia*) says the same thing. During the summer of 1890, the French and British quarrelled over these little desert islands. The British had planted their flag on the volcanic island of Perim, facing Aden, in order to close off our strait, which the Arabs call Bab-el-Mandeb. The stakes were high. Whoever could get his hands on the Suez Canal and the strait of Mandeb would control the shipping of oil across the Red Sea. That is why the French and the British were within an inch of setting off a war throughout the region and beyond—from Alexandria to Bombay, from Persia to Mozambique. It is truly the lust for blood that runs the world, Grandpa Assod would snigger.

The French wanted to turn the Devil's Islets into a rudimentary penal colony a thousand miles from nowhere. The English, into a munitions depot or something of the sort. Our ancestors had no say in the matter. At any rate, the locals—fishermen from Yemen or nomads from here—have no great love for those few acres of basalt. If Europeans from the other side of the world were fighting over those little volcanic islands, they had to be stark raving mad, and no brighter than the dumbest species of genies, our forefathers had concluded with a knowing smile. Needless to say, the French won the game.

That's how the Vichy regime, which was in charge of the colony in Grandpa Assod's day, had converted one of the two islets into an internment camp to keep the 'rebellious elements' away from the rest of the population of French Somaliland. The expression 'rebellious elements' was flexible and arbitrary. It referred to anyone who rebelled against abuses, humiliations and the draft. Very quickly the members of another species of whites called 'Germans' were interned there. They'd had the misfortune of being caught in France. Confined in makeshift hiding places, they'd been trying to survive by fleeing the officers of the Gestapo, not to mention the French police and gendarmes and hordes of collaborators. In vain. Little groups of them—ten, twenty or thirty—arrived here every three to four weeks from the summer of 1939 onwards. They were starving and shivering as if they had gone through a northern winter. And yet the trip from Marseille to Djibouti with a stopover at Suez bore no resemblance to a dash into Siberia. Resentment and hatred between the French and the other species of whites called 'Jehmann' was the least of my forefathers' worries. They knew the earth was overpopulated and the only thing that all living beings do is fight and tear each other apart relentlessly. And thus, since the dawn of time, men are born, they take out their daggers, devour each other and die, whereas only the serpent has the faculty of being born again after death. The serpent never dies, Grandpa Assod would say as he fearfully and respectfully stepped over the tiniest little worm or the slightest lizard dislodged from behind an embankment. Never trust the serpent that lies motionless, with flabby body and glassy eye. You think it's dead, whereas it's been eating dirt to regain its strength and return to life even stronger.

Memory functions more or less in the image of the serpent in my grandfather's story: when you think it's lost, it recovers all its energy. Now I can understand why that damned penal colony they installed on Devil's Islets and recently turned into a high-security prison haunted me well before I left Quebec. In the film of my childhood, I had already come across it at least twice. The first time in my grandfather's colonial stories, the second during my walks with David on Siesta Beach, exactly at the spot where my white twin was engaged in his letter-writing. Everything was becoming clear: the person who signed those mysterious letters could only be the last prisoner of the Pétain regime still alive at the time of my childhood. Had he been forgotten there by the French authorities? Had he become a misanthrope who chose to live as a recluse on his little island with cactus and wild hares for all company? Who knows?

●

Ha

So what do you know, you went on an expedition to
the islands. O you trickster from McGill, you wanted
to get close to us! And to do what? To look through
your binoculars and take snapshots of our jail from
every angle? Enjoy our banishment? Whoever wants
to drown his past is doomed to relive it; you should
know that better than I do, right? Can one bury a
secret so deep that the truth never comes to light
again?

And then, you went back to Djibouti, like a coward. Yesterday you lingered for a long time on Siesta
Beach. And you thought you could shake off the soldiers of God! I wouldn't have expected that from you.
You're pathetic. You are like them. You are worse
than them. From now on you are a prisoner of the
powers of evil that swallowed the region in a deluge of
fire in the ancestral eras. You are consumed with
envy, greed and the spirit of revenge. You never
should have left your territory of unbelief, your *dar al
kufr*, and set foot on this land again.

It looks like you're trying to lose yourself. You are behaving like an incoherent man who wants to ruin his life and uses the language of the traitors. In Mogadishu you would have been doused in petrol and burned in public. But what do you think? Of course we know all about you! You call your Canadian woman every night around 7 p.m., don't you? She talks a lot. She likes history books. She is a child psychologist. She has no offspring, for Divine Providence has decided otherwise, so she has transferred all her affection onto you. Am I wrong?

We are closely monitoring your every move. We know all about you, the cover of your bedside book and the brand of your toothpaste. Every word you say is reported to us, all the way to this watertight cell. A high-security prison, watched over day and night by a detachment of the presidential guard backed by elements of the infantry corps of the American Navy.

I am giving you these details so you can write them down in your ten little notebooks. If you were lucky enough to speak to him, my venerable Master would also point out to you that we are more closely watched than Ayman al-Zawahiri and his companions when they were imprisoned and tortured in Egyptian jails.

Your daydreams, your hesitations, your moods . . . they all reach us here. Yes, all the way to 'terrorist HQ', as they call it. Nothing escapes our organization. Our rules of discretion and our efficacy have been amply tested. It's no secret that our organization is built on the same model as other, far older and more prestigious organizations born in Egypt, Palestine and Kashmir, or amid immigrant communities. We attack our enemies valiantly and relentlessly. Once bitten, twice as resolute.

I have to admit that if it were only up to me you'd already be six feet under. But you lose nothing by waiting. We'll take care of you in two or three days, before your departure, which you would like to hasten. Everyone knows you would like to leave this country as quickly as possible and throw yourself into the arms of that sterile Zionist woman. You would run like a madman and rush into the belly of the Boeing. And our laughs and grimaces would follow you on the tarmac.

For the moment, we have far more urgent things to do, disciples to train, ground to prepare. What is more, the attentive examination of our glorious past requires our full attention. You know nothing about it, I am sure: our societies were thrown off track to serve the political, economic and spiritual interests of other groups. It stares you in the face, except for those who continue to stick their heads in the sand, as in Djibouti. My venerable Master would ask you: Are these cities really ours? These warehouse cities— yesterday ports for the coal mines, today cities of oil refineries and lust, cities of barracks? Were they ever ours? Aren't they only good for hiring mercenaries and askaris who will fight for someone else, far from their own lands? Aren't they only good for providing prostitutes to pamper the merchants, missionaries and soldiers who trampled on our land for the greater glory of the Western empires?

What a diabolical plan, while our populations have been banished to the desert where they rot, victims of eternal humiliations, eternal betrayals, and condemned to eternal misery! Do we not deserve better than this? Yes, much better. Is it not time to tell our people this truth, which is still more bitter today than it was yesterday? Those who answer in the affirmative will begin to open their eyes. They will hold their heads high and refuse to accept international aid which is supposed to be so generous. Their state of dependency will become unbearable to them and they will come join our ranks. They will burn down the rich people's neighbourhoods on their way. How many houses burnt to ashes with their balconies, living rooms and jewellery showing off their owner's high status? Sometimes the leg of a silenced piano will be lying there in the ruins, along with champagne glasses that have stayed in their box since the last passage of the French ambassador staggering between the legs of the courtesans, the opium pipes and the Istanbul flowerpots.

If, like me, you were lucky enough to drink in his words, my venerable Master would show you that in their day great minds like Hassan al-Banna and Sayyib Qutb left us luminous pages on the decadence of Nasser's Egypt and of an earlier time, when Gustave Flaubert, burning with fever from advanced syphilis, made his last visit to our lands. He would tell you that our brilliant writers and artists who followed the path of Joseph Kessel or André Gide finally ended up with no other choice but the asylum or the bottle. The living dead will never be creative—you should know that, shouldn't you? There's no point blaming exile or snow: they were already dead before they left their country. The living dead create nothing because they live in a whirlwind of abstractions, far from reality. They know nothing because they share nothing. All they believe in is their own pipe dreams. Their bodies breathe as ours do, but don't be fooled by it: those people aren't people like us. They are not filled with love for the Most Merciful, with compassion for their neighbours and generosity to the poorest. They scorn our values and our ways. They will find no peace: not by their mothers' side, nor in the shade of our cities. They will wander like you through a senseless world. They will live out their lives in the absence of being.

'Let them all go to hell!' My white-hot voice rose from my throat of its own volition, speaking of those eunuchs.

'Let them pay the full price of their mistrust!' my venerable Master cut in passionately.

At the precise moment I noticed my Master's vehemence—he who is usually so calm—my pen stumbled upon another writing for the first time. I did know that the pages I had at hand were not immaculately white. Certainly, I had noticed scribbles here and there, bits of words which I was able to cover up with my black ink. Once or twice it seemed to me these bits of words formed sentences, and these sentences came together to give birth to a paragraph. Up to now I had not yet encountered two or three paragraphs that followed each other to form something like coherent speech or fragments of a story. I am afraid that this is no longer true. Apparently fate has already decided otherwise.

The handwriting is tiny, so tiny it is hard for the human eye to follow those spikes and threads of ink. Is it not said that one can put the ninety-nine names of the All Powerful inside a grain of rice? By straining my eyes hard, I first managed to decipher the tiny letters twisting into each other like the fig and olive tree described in the sura *at-Tin*. I kept at it day after day. Now I can decode it at a reasonable rate and thus get into the story that was there before I took my dictation.

For the moment, it seems advisable to remain silent about the existence of these furrows of ink, or my august Master with the severe eyebrows would be displeased. Thank God, I still have a few pieces of paper on which to record our venerable Master's thoughts and teachings. He has just waved to indicate that the dictation is over. He is leaving, at least in thought: for in our dark room, space to retire and reflect is cruelly lacking.

We do not only lack air. We lack all that constitutes the banality of ordinary lives. I have learned never to complain for all is in the hands of the Divine. Soon it will be time for noonday prayer. I am getting ready to roll up my pages and store them away in their hiding place: a hole I dug in the loose earth, under my pillow. However, I can't bring myself to take my eyes off the first two pages, for I have succeeded in penetrating the secret of that writing. Surely there are secrets more difficult to unveil. All I had to do was bring the page under my nose and blow on it. Is not the human breath celebrated in many verses and Hadith? Believe it or not, after a few vain attempts my breath performed a miracle, or was it simply the effect of the air, so heavily saturated with iodine? Zones that at first seemed free of writing changed colour.

Now they are darkening, invading the page. Curves appear. Streaks are turning into rectilinear lines. Sentences are born and agglutinate to form paragraphs, and then pages. I strain my eyes while the beads of the rosary flow like big tears between my Master's fingers. His mind is wandering and his lips are moving. His thoughts come out linked together like verses. I raise my head. Perfumed scents—figs and pepper trees, jasmine and capers, will stay ripe for a few more days—arise from the land around us, and by the grace of The Compassionate, come in and tickle our nostrils.

I glance at the patriarch and then sink into the mirror that the other writing is holding out to me. I stroke its title with my finger. It is hardly legible, although intact.

The Book of Ben

. . . so here you are, Ben! I had been waiting for you for years. I knew our paths would cross one day or another. You arrived at that infamous camp in handcuffs, I remember it well; you had a vacant look about you. And already you longed to sew the broken pieces of our present back together again. They also say that in just a few weeks you had become Parisian to the hilt. In the city of Marcel

Proust, it's not harmony you were after, but the beauty of ordinary days. I also heard that your stories never ended at dawn (illegible scribble) . . .

. . . to tell the truth, I didn't know you personally, or at least not yet. But I had a pretty good picture of you because of all the stories that went around about you, the myriads of tales spread by word of mouth. Many narratives drawn from your life and work are circulating all over the world today. I brought those anonymous stories—those little autonomous vessels—along with me, all the way to the Horn of Africa . . . (big ink-blots) . . . I am turning to you because as fate would have it, our two paths happened to meet, by chance, in that internment camp in the south of France. And so for three weeks we shared fear, backbreaking work and stale bread. I was a dissident, you were a Jewish intellectual, but we were both German (grease spots) . . .

. . . I'm an old man now. I doubt that my nickname 'The Limping Angel' will mean anything to you. Ever since our chance encounter you have never left my mind. All I need is a pen and a piece of paper to find myself in your wake again. I imagine you better from far away than if I were with you, in Paris for instance. With a little effort I can see you clearly. As usual, you're going to unpack your library. One by one, you'll take out your books. But there won't be enough space for them, your room is so cramped. There are already books, manuscripts and newspapers on the bed, piled on the floor, heaped up everywhere. The very first day in this tiny Paris apartment, you religiously tacked up Paul Klee's *Angelus Novus* on the wall right in front of the small work table. It is your good-luck charm, your missal, your prophylactic talisman. Your terribly myopic eyes lose their way as they strive to reach that horizon. And you throw yourself into your work. You make a pretence of working. In vain. Your shoulders show whether you're inspired or not. You try again but something resists you. You remain motionless for a long time, your hand on your cheek. You ruminate, you turn words around and around in your mouth like an olive pit stuck under your tongue. A strange sterility for someone who used to say that 'Paris is the great reading room of a library crossed by the Seine.' Can all of life be contained in a reading room? In forty-eight years, all you have done is read and write. 'That's all he's good for,' said your childhood friend Gershom Scholem, the future exegete of the Torah at the University of Jerusalem (faded ink-blots) . . .

I keep stroking that strange title over and over with my finger. It seems magical to me.

●

The Smell of the Father

My boss called me at dawn. I didn't have the time to drink my glass of water as I usually do. Still less to boot up my computer. He was impatient. Concerned, too.

'You should go right to the mark without losing sight of the international context, Djib. We have a timetable to follow. Are you listening? You should get into it now, this is the ideal time!'

That's what the former student of cultural anthropology at Stanford was exhorting me to do.

I explained that the situation on the ground was extremely tense.

'We're well aware of that,' he cut in sharply, before brusquely going into the strategy of the mullahs of Teheran, who skilfully combine Persian imperial tradition and contemporary Islamic fervour.

I stammered out a few excuses, as I didn't have the time to ask what he was getting at with these reflections about Iran. Everybody knows the country has built electronuclear installations, like Pakistan and North Korea, and has entered the race for mineral deposits right here in Africa. What did he mean? Is Teheran once again in the crosshairs of the hawks in the Pentagon or is this simply an echo of their usual paranoia? He hung up on me. I was furious and powerless.

I took advantage of the brief morning coolness and set out for a madrasa buried in the colossal garbage dump of Damerjog, in the south of the country. There I met two people who had been recommended to me. The lead had been indicated to me by a well-paid informer. What they said was incoherent and their hypotheses, idle. Believers in the Jewish conspiracy. Denigrators of Israel: you can find thousands of them between the Sahel and the Sahara. I realized very quickly that nothing solid would come from these interviews. So as not to arouse their suspicions, I took abundant notes, ripe for the garbage can. I nodded at every one of their questions while pretending to confirm or deny the bit of information in question. You'd think they were put on my trail to make me waste my time. This is the kind of detail that makes an investigation take shape or dissolve under your very eyes.

There is nothing I like less than ruminations. I am paid—and rather well—to investigate and judge the reliability of testimony, establish evidence and bring back the results of my observation.

My sponsors are impatient, as only great financial experts who are constantly selling and finishing off whole countries can be. They have no use for my procrastination and tears over my former life.

And yet no one goes over the traces of his childhood without cost. My father left in me certain sensations I will never forget, certain images engraved on the low sky of my memories. His skeleton-white hair. His bony carcass. His rigid walk, which made you think something in his spine had become irreparably stuck. He had to compensate for the stiffness of his back by making big movements with his hips. I've kept in my memory an incident which often haunted me later on. I was in a bus coming back from school, surrounded by my noisy friends. My brother, whom I saw only now and then, was excused from class that day because he was having some tests done at the hospital. Suddenly I saw my father, walking along the mosque that goes down to the biggest square in the city. And I felt ashamed of that man, ashamed of his crab-like steps and jerky walk. Of his poverty, too. He was on foot, whereas I would have liked to see him at the wheel of a Peugeot—even a beat-up Peugeot. He was bringing back a box-spring mattress that we didn't have at home. He was carrying it on his head, probably to save the price of a collective taxi. He was walking slowly, with an impassive face. At every step he would nearly collapse on his mattress, which was light but very bulky. My friends' laughter thundered around me. I did not get off to help him. I turned my head away, afraid that a friend might notice my embarrassment—or worse still, recognize my father. I was almost grown-up and I was ashamed of him. I am the son of that shame and I was to remain imprisoned in it until the end of my days.

The impressions that are most certain to shape you are those you absorb early, unconsciously. As if shame, that monstrous ape, ate away at my guts, amputated one of my limbs or made me fatherless. I was unable to accept it or pretend to ignore it. I know I'm going to carry around that vile feeling stewing in the depths of my guts wherever I go. I must learn to live with it.

Fifteen years later, have I overcome that shame? I doubt it. Ashamed of his rags, of his faltering health, of his disjointed walk. There are kinds of shame one never forgets. In the quick life of the present as in the eddies of the past, they accompany me everywhere.

Strangely, my morning wasn't a total loss. The two guys I'd met at Damerjog had nonetheless put me on the trail of a woman. A European, a former interpreter for UNESCO. A Frenchwoman, apparently caught in the web of a plot that went far beyond her. Did they release this piece of information intentionally or was it the only one they had? Hard to decide. The informers didn't seem very sure of their act. I took the bus back. I got to the hotel early enough to get Montreal before noon, local time. The muezzin was calling the faithful to the prayer of the 'Asr, at the end of the afternoon. I went over the situation with Denise from my room. Far off in Montreal, she was able to help me create a rigorous file on the informers, classify it, archive it and check it against other elements. She has a formidable gift for steering me through the labyrinth of my hypotheses and forcing me to redefine my priorities. Afterwards, I had a light dinner—cheese plate and salad—lying on my bed, an eye on CNN and Al Jazeera English.

And yet very quickly, I took off. A singular levitation. The closeness of Siesta Beach is probably reason enough for the past to shelter me under its wing. I felt the little voice of my childhood well up in me, mixed with David's voice on the beach. Now both of us are sitting elbow to elbow in front of the sea, as we used to do.

I still can see us today in that position. Two little bodies squeezed together, trembling with joy. Two ill-matched twins, smiling and silent. My brother Djamal had instinctively understood that a trio would always lead to conflict. Every time we ran into him, he looked more unhappy than the previous day. He said he was ill, giving the impression that he had a stone in his stomach and a porcupine in his throat. I did not feel sorry for him.

●

Kha

Well, well, what's this I hear? The kafir from Quebec can't keep still, am I right? You went to the south. And you beat a retreat the first chance you got. Like a yellow-belly, you sealed yourself in your hotel room all evening long. And you had a long phone conversation with your psychologist wife, or partner as you say in America. You said yes to everything she said, to all her questions. Now just listen to this story, it concerns you. It concerns all of us. It is not a pretty oriental tale, as you'll soon see. Let me guide you now, oh you, Djibril the mollusc!

Once upon a time there were twelve cities blessed twelve times over. Twelve cities which had been endowed with all the favours of the earth by the grace of The Compassionate. Now one day, out of defiance or carelessness, they wandered off the true path. How can one turn away from this ancient faith, everywhere victorious, to seek refuge in the palaces and alcoves of lust? How can one forget that the earth belongs to God (may His name be ceaselessly sanctified) and that He has lent it to us for our daily survival for a very limited time? How can they take themselves for the owners of this passing, temporary life which has been allotted to us and should be devoted entirely to His praise? How can they forget the law of our fathers to the point of no longer circumcising their offspring?

To think that our fathers crossed and re-crossed the Sinai, their only land passage between the two continents, Africa and Asia; that they set up the caravan routes connecting China to Syria through India and Persia all the way to Lake Chad. The progress in navigation—blessed be the monsoon and the trade winds—made our task easier. And thus we were able to carry the word of Allah further still. We brought the pagans back to the right direction, destroying their idols and building mosques on the very sites of their crimes, elevating their spirits and improving their daily life through our masters, who continued their work amid these populations. Our message and our power stretched over the seven seas and the five continents, bringing peace and progress to a thousand tribes who had only known raids and ruins. No wonder the mere name of one of those cities aroused envy and fear, rekindling in our vassals old injuries long repressed.

That is what we used to be, repeated the Master before clearing his throat to take up the thread of his sermon once again, which allowed me to wipe my hands on a corner of my djellaba and get back to taking dictation.

Our ancestors had the clear feeling that God had assembled those twelve cities to see them accomplish extraordinary actions or experience an exemplary decline. Little by little, they lost their splendour. Inertia paralyzed their august commanders who preferred to look back at their past glory. They were more prompt to commemorate and sing the great deeds of yesterday than confront the diktats of the present. From then on, poverty prowled through our cities, a foreign passenger at first but increasingly familiar as time went by. Arbitrary power and violence, looting and thieving became the norm. Swarms of locusts descended on the fields of our farmers, precipitating flight from the land. Our Bedouins died by the thousands in the desert. Dark ruminations and prophecies black as mourning arose everywhere. The sultans lost their aura and their honour, wallowed in debauchery, carried on openly with impious mistresses who kept looking out for the good of their own country. From season to season, all the values that made the reputation of our region, like hospitality, piety, generosity and the work ethic had become incantations at best, shameful and old-fashioned at worst. One after the other, the twelve cities fell into utter disarray. Even words lost their meaning.

Believe me, dear pious pupils, this is what happened. It is not because I am a good storyteller that this tale is so dark, God be my witness.

I raised my head and looked at my Master who was seized by a fit of coughing. I prayed that he would not suffocate. I raised my two clasped hands to heaven, imploring The Benefactor. A silence followed, my prayers were granted. Amin Allahu! My Master was breathing normally. And at the moment my eyes settled on my piece of paper again, I had the clear sensation that the other writing had already resurfaced . . .

The Book of Ben

... it is dark at this time of the afternoon. The Paris sky is suffused with an autumnal atmosphere. I can see you as if I were there. Yes, I see you glued to your table as you have been every day of your life. I turn to you. You have in your hands a children's book illustrated by Marc Chagall. Then, you go back to your notebook. Its pages breathe out the scent of the past before you even turn them. They are dirty yellow, and the writing is invisible in certain spots, as if worn away and swallowed up by the sun. This notebook has not been opened in many years. It was left with the old Jewish hat-maker of Rosenthaler Platz or hidden in a drawer in the apartment of some casual lover. And you thought it was lost when you moved from one place to another in Berlin. You tremble as you turn those pages, you stumble at the threshold of your memory. You are afraid they might reveal something unbearable. Something you had succeeded in burying. This notebook is a mosaic of notes. Succinct notes, a series of words that make an impression. Filled with repetitions and the obsessions of the deeply melancholy man that you are. Those pages say all there is to know about you. Your fears, your sorrows and your illnesses. You have remained an introvert, whereas all around you the other exiles talk loudly and shout; half their words die on their lips as soon as they come out. (hole in the page) . . .

. . . and we are living through uncertain times, but the Devil is here, that professional prowler. Locking up his captives, more numerous than stars in a moonless sky. A few of us are doing our utmost to ward off the many maledictions that threaten us, first by remaining alive and then by spreading the word from hill to hill, from village to village, from town to town, from island to island. What happiness to see perfect strangers thrill when they meet us, to hear the first wails come out of their throats, their first sounds being born on their tongue and becoming clusters of sounds and then words that bring hope. Among those whose lips are already moving perhaps there will be one or two individuals—children, most often—who will defy all that is forbidden, leave their group, face the darkness, save their fellow men and spread the word far and wide. They will survive through the ages. They are united by a simple, solid, fleshly pact. That is how things happened . . .

As I read and reread these fragments, an extravagant idea comes to me: Was the author of these writings of the same breed as I am? Was he performing the same task? Could he be a scribe who writes down everything that is dictated to him—or a liar who makes up whatever he wants? What do you have to say about that, you imposter from the far north?

●

The Man with Two Graves

I turn off my computer and slip my new notebook into the drawer. Reassured by the fact that a thief wouldn't get much from my notes, which are legible for no one except Denise, I leave my hotel perkily. I'm even whistling.

From the steps of the hotel, I notice barely perceptible changes in this privileged part of the city which has a peninsular look to it. The road disappears under the sand in some places. The potholes in the roadway grow bigger and suddenly come together, swallowing up the asphalt in an animal hug. The sidewalks are nonexistent, drowned in mud. As I leave the city on a road that goes up the side of a cliff, the ground becomes increasingly rocky and turns the colour of brick as soon as the sun is no longer at its zenith. It is inside this perimeter that the charred corpse of the French judge Bernard Borrel was found on 18 October 1995. The affair has poisoned relations between

Djibouti and France ever since. Suicide? Murder? The mystery has not been solved to this day. French counter-espionage came up empty. Perhaps the CIA or MI5 will offer their services to clear up the enigma.

No point leaving the comfort of my taxi, rented for half a day; I know instinctively how hard it can be to walk around here. You have to imitate the goats and hop over the volcanic stones that cut into the soles of your feet and twist your ankles. Under your shoes, the black pebbles make a sound like broken china. A column of smoke is rising to the east, in the direction of the airport. A military convoy back from an operation in the backcountry? The wind brings back the twin smell of sulphur and salt. A few weeks ago a portion of earth collapsed on the other bank of the Gulf under the power shovels that wound the crust of the earth, thinner here than a millet pancake. Nature chips in, too. The wind catapulted the stones into the very bottom of Goubet al-Kharab. We learned later that the sea was acting up because of the tsunami. Four thousand cubic metres of stones and dirt slid into the sea in just a few minutes. It's the domino theory: a flutter of butterfly wings above the Amazon forest is enough to set off a hurricane right here in the Gulf of Tadjoura.

I don't know if the nomads have a solid explanation for this kind of phenomenon.

Grandpa Assod was a born storyteller. When his stories took hold of him, his voice would take on a tense, obsessive rhythm. He came into the world in a nomad camp with some unknown name half a century before our birth. I opened my eyes inside the intimate perimeter of what would become my playground. My beloved neighbourhood. Three or four streets, no more. The lake of my life, mud-coloured when things are going badly, the colour of hibiscus when the sun is shining in the hearts of men. Already I liked to imagine myself observing the world through the glassy eye of my mother's womb. 'Little Brother' wasn't there yet. I was prince of the world for a good half hour. It was said that I had a bulging navel and sluggish knees at birth. I recall one thing perfectly: the humidity of the air in the courtyard. It was so sticky that the skinny little fan which was unconvincingly stirring the air couldn't manage to dissipate the humidity. They had then washed my eyes, ears, nostrils and anus. Once free from impurities, shining like a new penny, I focused my thoughts on the woman who had engendered me. I contemplated the high solitudes of human pastures. I could pray in silence despite the soggy heat of the city which was about to be mine. All around me, they were speaking some kind of pidgin disguised as Somali. Onomatopoieas and gurglings looped back at me constantly. Why didn't they talk like everybody else? Why did they insist on thinking in lazy thoughts? I had the feeling of lying in front of a cactus wall. Without admitting it to myself, my resistance to my family had already begun.

As a child, I got into the habit of covering my back, of defending my crust of bread with the barbarousness born of despair. Once I had secured food and drink, I would give myself over to anticipations and projections. I had predicted that the country would go nowhere and the fathers would sink into twilight. Only strong ladies who'd had their dose of all the nastiness of life would survive without ever losing their dignity. At that time, Mother was already getting up at dawn whereas Father would often sleep till noon.

I was serious then, even grave, but I would nonetheless indulge in the petty thefts of children my age.

It was like a second skin, or, if you prefer, a chameleon costume—a cover to prevent suspicion. I also knew my limits and kept one eye on the doings of 'Little Brother.' I never ran away, never deserted. Nor did I push recklessness to the point of joining the ranks of the kids who lost their heads sniffing gasoline, glue or *white spirit* out of Pepsi-Cola cans. I was saving myself for the great missions to come, the investigations to conduct, mysteries to solve and heroic pages to write. For the moment, just petty thefts; and from time to time an impromptu raid on the back room of Uncle Farah's shop. With the change I lifted I would buy myself a paper cone full of peanuts or hot spicy fritters. Grandpa Assod, whom I'd run into on my way out of the shop, would immediately worry:

'Where're you going like that? And your brother—where's he? Don't run so fast, little lion!'

The words were droned out for a long time before being set down on Koranic plates. The *muallim* of the madrasa was not always tyrannical. Not in my memories, at least. He called you 'numbskull' every time you deserved it and that was that. If he scolded someone, it was my twin brother, who was quicker to rebel than I was. Little by little, our *muallim* had turned away from the moving walkway of life. He had accepted his meagre lot and was waiting for the ordinary death which would not fail to come in due course.

A short eternity later, we were kicking a soccer ball around, hard. There were as many of us on the playing field as young fish on Doraleh beach. We yelled loudly. We made a circle around the dribbler. Between the two of us, my brother and I could keep possession of the ball better than all the other players put together. A pass to you, a pass to me. And goal. When the game was over, we pretended to build our muscles by lifting cooking utensils filled with water by the little maid of the household.

At last we had access to writing and artistic expression: we would take a fat piece of chalk and scribble idiocies, insults and shameless words—the ones we thought were the worst. From then on we knew school French. *Moi j'enquile ta seur pour 10F*: 'I fok your sista inna ass for ten francs,' one would invent. And the other would immediately add 'alway' by way of signature. The brothers of the sister whose honour was tarnished would try to find the author of the crime to the end of their days.

The indigo meadows of childhood return to me in memory, and so do the burning colours of adolescence, which people always celebrate a bit too much. The saffron afternoons cannot be forgotten either. Times when the moon is a golden fingernail in a shimmering sky. As long as death isn't in your home it's striking the neighbour's, taught Grandpa Assod, making an old proverb his own. And starting from the intimate perimeter of my neighbourhood, we would make complicated calculations to determine the exact spot where death was prowling. I must confess, now that time has done its job and I hardly feel that childish shame any more, that sometimes we would make a mistake: we would dispatch an old man of the neighbourhood from God's earth, for example. In short, we instinctively measured the import of a proverb we did not yet know at the time. For death is not always an equation with three unknowns. Rather, in those times it had the face of a familiar animal. In our family nest alone, out of five children with a scarred belly button, three had left as soon as they arrived. Little sisters we would never know. Death had to pass through our house every three years. And that was it. Not to mention a sickly father about whom the whole neighbourhood had real reasons to worry, as well as a distant, taciturn mother. And members of our clan driven from the bush that had fed them, by drought, cattle epidemics or war; they would give up their guts and their phlegm in the court-yard. Meanwhile death had a lot to do in the area. You could follow its track. All you had to was notice the tents set up for funerals. Here, some little guy was returning to the depths of emptiness . . . Besides, he was never referred to as 'dead' but 'gone back'—*shafeec* in the language of our people. There, some cripple went from life to death: the Grim Reaper had surprised him in the middle of his evening prayer. There again, a young man, about thirty and apparently in good health, had left us with no warning whatsoever. They said he stumbled and broke his heart. A madwoman had set herself on fire in the square in front of the mosque on the pretext that the Demon kept winking at her emphatically. This time around she would be saved and everyone would exclaim that her part of the cake was spared, it was written on high, and death itself could do nothing about it. Karim Allahu!

Stranger still was the case of the man-with-two-graves. He had twice been given up for dead but he was still among us. The last time, they had brought him back from the morgue. They had washed, cleaned and purified him. The proper prayers had been said for him in the neighbourhood mosque. Then, his grave was dug in the middle of the nearest cemetery. At the last minute, someone had detected a little breath that was surreptitiously raising his cold chest. Life was sneaking back into him; his body had warmed, turning from stiffened wood to living flesh, though still quite numb. Some said his right thumb had moved. Others retorted that he had opened an eye. And what followed was a mass of theories and speculations. Some said he had mumbled a sura. Others supposedly made out the name of his wife Khadidja on his lips. Still others claimed he had pronounced words incomprehensible to men in these parts. Only one thing is certain—his stupefied family immediately started back home with this adage on their lips:

'When it's not your time, it's really not your time!'

'He'll bury us all, I'm telling you—me, Ayoub.'

'Let's go away, that man already has two graves.'

'Laba Qabrileh will still live among us. It is the will of the Lord.'

'We bow down before Allah, poor microbes that we are!'

'Amin!'

In our dreams we imagined ourselves stronger, taller, and above all fatter. We would scratch our stomachs and stroke our chins before belching with pleasure. Kids with soft flesh and fat thighs were taunted as much as they were envied. We would fling in their face the names of the brands of powdered milk their mothers used at home: 'Go back to your bowl of milk, you greedy son-of-a-Nido!' was always the supreme insult, ranking second only to names for their mothers' intimate anatomy. Our childish babble was obsessed with eating, because Nature here rarely permits abundance. In fact, the shreds of grass that grew here could hang on to the blackish rock for no more than a handful of days. So it was goodbye rice, goodbye semolina! Goodbye yams, manioc and bananas! Goodbye potatoes, tomatoes and juicy mangoes! Goodbye sesame, watermelon and pomegranates!

The starving, furtive cats of my childhood knew something about that. Even today, between two short runs, they stop under a table, under a bench or against a wall to catch their breath.

●

Dal

Ah, you're going around in a taxi now! And you want us to think you're a great sleuth, an ace of military–industrial intelligence. Now, if I may, I shall resume the thread of my venerable Master's narrative.

And hope returned to our twelve cities, thanks to a new category of citizens—the same ones who not so long ago were considered foreigners, immigrants and refugees. Some of them, or their relatives, got organized, left the decadent cities and took over the grottoes and rocky shelters like Muhammad and His estimable Companions in the olden days. They set up camps in the desert and the savannah, gathered together all available men and revived faith in The Unique in all hearts. And they armed themselves as well, to defend themselves and reconquer the territories that had fallen into the hands of renegades and infidels.

My venerable Master's face is radiant at this moment. He has stopped coughing. I believe the thought of those first seeds of resistance still make him smile. They will bring forth the tree of renewal. I smile at him in return. We are all smiling. I wonder if he had felt the smile taking shape on my lips. It makes me lose the flow of the dictation. I have stumbled over a block of words.

Tradition tells us that in the time of our Prophet, the *ayats*, or verses, were written on several makeshift supports like palm leaves, pieces of leather, flat bones, pottery shards or stones. Then they were memorized by the believers. The death of one or several of those Companions with a prodigious memory led them, out of prudence, to compile suras that brought together the revelations the Prophet had received from the messenger, the angel Djibril. This is how we went from the spoken word to the written word—for the delectation of scribes like me. Our task has not always been easy. Right now, for instance, I feel helpless before this block of ink. For our divine book, the Holy Koran, also called the summa of books, *Umm al-Kitab*, constantly asks us deficient creatures to strive for perfection by devoting ourselves night and day to The Dominator. I am attracted by the black mass that has taken shape under my very eyes. There is absolutely no doubt about it: another writing is there. Another story is waiting to be delivered, in its turn. As if the hand of a second scribe were taking over the dictation, the thread of my narrative, and propelling it in a completely different direction. As if a second storyteller were secretly biding his time. Another storyteller, known only to me. My accomplice . . .

The Book of Ben

. . . no, Ben, you never were very chatty. I like calling you Ben, it's more intimate and less intimidating than Dr Walter Benjamin. The rare words that can come out of your mouth seem held back by a mysterious force. Then they crash against our eardrums like the dull thud of a swallow smashing into a window. They reveal the darkness of the past, the harmonies lost in the heart of Europe or the magic of deep woods.

Half the population of Czernowitz, that Romanian city in the Bukovina region, is Jewish. It is a prosperous town that does have its quota of poor people. A powerful bastion of Western culture that lasted, year in year out, until the middle of the last century. Paul Celan was born there in 1920; he was two years younger than your only son, Stefan.

The silent zone is a territory of the imagination where anything is possible. It is similar to a desert in which only century-old cacti are slowly blooming, their spines raised towards infinity. Your eyes are reflected, Ben, in the mirror of other eyes; your silence fills other bodies. And you have not forgotten the face of your father the antique-dealer, the scents of your wealthy bourgeois household, the shine of the silverware, the fine furniture. If you miss a detail, it's up to us to read between the lines and fill in the blanks. But how could you forget the games of childhood, the radiant moments like the bike rides through the gardens of Tiergarten in the company of lovely Anja with her delicate features; and the fights with Egon, that kid with an old man's face; your walks along the banks of the Spree whose deep waters are the colour of drowning; the conversations with your hobbyhorse in the large family living room, and your friendship with the old hat-maker straight out of the Book of Moses.

A blazing sky, the furnace of an eternal summer, intermittently showed its face in place of the usual mists. You were handsome then. Handsome as an Italian prince who'd stepped out of one Venetian painting to walk into another. All that is so far away. As far off as the time when humanists could master thirteen or fourteen languages. As far away as the time when men had laid the first stone of the city of your birth. Berlin: two exotic syllables on a plain swept by freezing winds. A face of wax out of an ancient story. Berlin of all the workers drumming the beat of the Industrial Revolution. Berlin: your winding shape glinting with pitch and amber, summoning the enchantments of old Europe before toppling into the camp of death.

It was in the smoke-filled cafes of Berlin that you first began to write, under the influence of the Romantics and utopians of the century before ours, already in tatters.

You wrote so much about the history of your country, about the twilight of the empire and the gleaming fires of the Weimar Republic. You drew from myths, Judaism and the arts. You were a poet who gave flesh to inexpressible things, somewhat as Joseph Roth did, another poet and pilgrim much like yourself. You lost yourself for a while in a forest as lush as the archipelago of the German language—far richer, far more complex and more flexible than its Latin neighbours. You emphasized the capacity of that language to retain its mystery until the end of the sentence. To you, that language which struggles with ancient metaphysical questions of time, existence, dream and reality was always a source of pride. You will keep it alive to the end of your wanderings from Denmark to the labyrinthine islands of the Mediterranean and up to the border of the Pyrenees. To the end of your sojourn among men . . .

●

'Confession,' You Said?

Back in my room, a message was waiting for me. A man who claimed to have some information had left me a note. He had used the word 'confessions' in the email he'd sent me the week before, first to my professional address. I had almost forgotten this individual. The term 'confession' had intrigued me right away. I thought for a while the word 'confession' was blinking on the screen of my laptop. The rest of the message was brief. Two lines indicating the time and meeting place, 'as soon as you arrive in Djibouti,' he said. Why such impatience? I had attributed his saying 'confession' to his imperfect mastery of the language: the guy must have watched a spy movie the night before, where some James Bond imitator was taking the confession of a double agent. Unless it was about some kind of treasure hunt. In that case we would be like two Kabbalists: one who writes and one who reads. Two Kabbalists engaged in a very playful

tête-à-tête. One who provokes and one who reacts.
One who gives information and one who decodes it.
We would be the only ones capable of understanding
the significance of this word or that. That's what I'd
thought before I reached my room and immersed
myself in the investigation of the past and present of
the Devil's Islets.

I have less than two days left. My investigation is
making no headway, and this throws me into a terrible state. Luckily, I'm not always so glum. Sometimes
I burst out laughing as I go through my documenta-
tion. Like when I happened to come upon a leaflet
calling for the conquest of Ethiopia by Mussolini's
troops. This leaflet was unearthed in the archives of
the French Foreign Office by a young historian at the
University of Djibouti which has just opened its
doors.

> *Gibuti a noi*! *Gibuti a noi*!
>
> The clamour skilfully orchestrated by
> the glorious army of our Duce, Mussolini, is
> rising from the Piazza Venezia in Rome.
> Djibouti is ours. Something never heard

before in Rome, where no one would be able to find this French colony on a map. Piazza Venezia, where the fascists assemble, is adamant about rectifying this situation. Nothing can resist the will of the great Duce. The moment has come to reconquer the magnificence of the Roman Empire, reshape the world in our glorious image and undo history. It is time to absolve the past, to rub out the old African wound. The wound still has a name: Aduwa. A name as aggressive as a toxic perfume. The wound has a face: Ethiopia, which defeated the Italian troops there in 1898 under Menelik II. Shame! *Che vergogna!* How could a bunch of backward little tyrants, led by a preposterous little emperor, humiliate the Italians before the whole world! Why should our strong nation be the only one to suffer a defeat in Africa, champ at the bit, and be denied colonies commensurate to its greatness? The country of Julius Caesar will hold its head high again and erase the legend of King Solomon and the Queen of Sheba from the pages of universal history. There is nothing more fraudulent than this chronicle culled from various archives and nothing more specious than the antics at the court of Menelik! Come, raise your heads, sons of Garibaldi! We will march on this pseudo-imperial palace.

Gibuti a noi! Gibuti a noi!

We will enter through Djibouti, Ethiopia's main outlet onto the Red Sea and the outside world. We will march on Djibouti, crush the French colonists and their army and starve out the natives: we hear they are not so numerous in this part of Africa, which is essentially a desert. The French are bound to flee as soon as they see our banners, and if they have any intention of fighting, we will make them surrender. And the French government, extremely preoccupied by the military situation on its eastern and southern fronts, will hesitate for days and weeks before deciding to send reinforcements. Our seasoned troops will make short work of them and then pounce on the elite corps of the army of Haile Selassie, the heir of Menelik. To leave gloriously, see the world, risk their skin if necessary to come closer to the Mother Country: that is what will motivate our young soldiers, who are devoted to our great leader Mussolini. Djibouti, what a strange name. A name strange as the dream of a repressed schoolboy, a call of the hot sirocco wind.

Djibouti the French, the British or the Italian? To talk like lovers of algebra, this unknown must be solved first. The second unknown is the following: Why here rather than elsewhere?

Why was the Bay of Djibouti so attractive to the Europeans? And what was Djibouti originally? A handful of little magical islands over which history rose and swirled like a hurricane for centuries? A handful of little islands like beauty spots on the neck of a beautiful woman rich in legends and rumours?

The islets can be seen when the fog rises, but most often, sailors go around them. They can be reached by magic only, at nightfall. Nothing makes them attractive. Everything is lacking in this bay except for a brackish well at ground level. Vegetation is nothing more than a coat of spiny plants that attracts the flocks. At all times there is a nasty smell of volcanic sulphur in the air that eats into your skin and your bones. It is said that wild hares had colonized the bay long before the arrival of the Yemeni sailors. In this same bay, south of the present capital, American forces set up a top-secret spy centre, as if they wanted to give credence to old legends. A wiretapping centre in the middle of nowhere may be surprising, but future events proved the American intelligence agencies right. And all that well before the attack on the USS Cole a few miles away in Yemeni waters on 12 October 2000. That American destroyer, a missile-launcher, was making a routine stop for refuelling in the port of Aden in the south of Yemen. Bad idea. Seventeen American sailors were killed in the explosion and thirty-eight wounded. The two perpetrators were also killed in the attack. Two years later, the French tanker Limburg suffered the same fate. According to *Asharq Al-Awsat*, a generally well-informed newspaper, a prisoner at Guantanamo named Walid ibnou Habash, alias Antar ibn Antar, alias Monsour al-Amriki—he studied biochemistry

in Richmond, Virginia, hence the imperialist nickname—has since declared that he bought explosives
and recruited the two men who blew up a small craft
against the port side of the ship.

These two attacks, not to mention the failed
attack on *The Sullivans*, another warship in the American Navy which was also passing through the port of
Aden in January 2000, demonstrated the usefulness
of this wiretap espionage centre, so discreet and so
precious.

●

Dhal

So, you mollusc from Quebec, you're holing up in your room now? You're dragging your feet, you're daydreaming away. Do you know that ghosts make their nests in the fractures of history? You think I have gone mad. It is also said that poets, bards and griots are often blind, unlike scribes such as your humble servant. It is said that they look into the minds of men, dig into the secret of their souls and succeed in soothing their conscience. It is well known that loss of sight stimulates the memory. The blind man can see far ahead of him. He perceives what makes life thrilling, and cannot be seen by ordinary men. The blind man is silent when he is not at work. The illness that afflicts the chatterbox is intemperance in language and the ability to produce sounds without listening to anyone, without affecting reality.

I am at present a little stammering scribe who has given himself to the Lord, who has found peace in his heart by His side. A copyist in the ancient style, older than Plutarch, wiser than Socrates or Ahmed Eqbal. I take down the dictation of my venerable Master who is, of course, blind. His words have the gift of crossing time and space without suffering too much damage. I only prolong their course a bit, like a particle accelerator. Geophysicists, specialists in tectonic plates, seismographers, vulcanologists and palaeontologists all came to our corner of Africa in quest of the secrets of the Earth. They scrupulously observed the upheavals of our good old terrestrial crust, measured infinity and space, and prognosticated the secrets of The Sublimely Exalted. How are volcanoes born? And what about oceans? Why do mummies decompose in the open air? Why this, why that? They finally came to the following truth: terra firma does not exist. It's a legend, good only for bucking up the morale of accountants and statisticians in need of certitudes.

Mountains are born, twist or collapse under the weight of glaciers without any scientific explanation. Why is there no life outside of our planet? Doesn't all science rest on this paradoxical silence? Hills grow and round off; valleys dip under streams or dry out. Not very far from here, an ocean is gestating. The plates are going to pull apart. The Horn of Africa is going to disappear under water. From this great drift, a small piece will remain in the middle of the Indian Ocean, according to divine will. A brand new island, which, of course, does not yet have a name. That is what they concluded. You were not aware of this? Denise didn't tell you yet? What a shame. But don't let that bother you. There is an explanation. I have it from my venerable Master to whom I yield always, even when he's wrong or his angry temperament plays tricks on him. We will not have the time to experience this drift of the continents. It will come in good time, with the help of the Ever-Providing.

Could this world here below be nothing but a clumsy improvisation? The old European powers sank into an ocean of decadence. The young nations that were scorned in former times are raising their heads, striving to ignite vast rebellions; but they have renounced their faith. The world today has been inverted: death precedes birth, the flower the bud, and the scar, the wound.

You never should have set foot in this country. In your opinion, is my Guide's blindness a gift or an ordeal? Only The Most Lofty knows. I must face facts: my Master is getting old! He is sometimes nasty and bitter. May The Compassionate give us new

strength to face his weaknesses! He hasn't stopped
coughing these past few days. My chest hurts as if I
were coughing instead of him. Ah! now I'm stumbling
over that damned palimpsest again . . .

The Book of Ben

. . . come over here, Ben, come here slowly.
You are short of breath, and move forward in
life with a heavy step. Your lips are moving.
You're talking to yourself, unless you're engaged in a dialogue with your guardian angel,
your double who follows you around like
your shadow, even here in this wretched
camp. True, everyone knows you hate official
saints, miraculous grottoes and beatific
angels, but no one understands why you
were still hanging around Paris when the
angels had deserted it. Who are you, Benjamin? A holy man unwinding the Ariadne's
thread of his conscience? A lonely, poly-
graphic chame-leon? A scholar afflicted with
an immense sadness, who's not sure of his
own talents? An extraordinary mind that
remembers everything? (Great philosophical

theories as well as slogans from the strikes of yesteryear and lullabies of his Berlin childhood hummed late into the night:

'No cash, no style

Just a big fat heart beating

A creamy heart!

A liquorice heart!')

We enter every new period of our lives with a blindfold on. You say nothing. That's exactly what worries me. Life will never resemble what we thought it would be in early childhood. Never.

You will meet your friends again and make up with the ones you kept at arm's length because you had fallen out with them. If you're lucky enough to get out of here, you'll have to leave Paris, and more certainly, the tiny apartment on Rue Dombasle: too cold in winter, too hot in summer. Not an ounce of oxygen in the air of that one room these past few days, a room the size of a phone booth—worse still, a booth on an uphill street. You don't complain about it because your mind is on other matters. You have too many things to do: write articles, formulate intuitions, tend the fire of your friendship with Gershom Scholem, elaborate theses and beg for your colleagues' acceptance like a dog for its collar. Already at twenty, you were constantly testing out your theoretical constructions on family and friends. Mischievously, you would expound your wackiest hypotheses to total strangers, people you passed on the street or met in cafes. Your eyes would light up when the result was convincing; when the opposite happened you would stroke your bushy mustache, groan for form's sake and then politely apologize before going on your merry way as if nothing had happened. And on the way back you would even dance like a dervish turning on himself, whirling under the quarter moon of a sky bursting with stars.

The Berlin of your childhood was synonymous with passion and effervescence.

That was yesterday, Ben, but you have the feeling it was very far away. So do I. The whole bunch of you used to fool around in all kinds of ways and duel with the enemy of the moment. You would also give each other nicknames—as affectionate or cutting as the edge of your pride.

Anja would tease you with '*Gatito*, my little cat!'

You would remain *Gatito* for that faithful comrade from those Marxist circles, your first political commitment. You must have been quite agile to deserve that feline nickname. You would sleep over at each other's place, reading, smoking and arguing all night long. You lived on black bread and Italian wine, you decided which paintings would be hung and shown for free. You all argued a lot, and when it rained, water would begin to drip from the ceiling before one of you tarred the roof to patch up the holes. Except for you, Ben, none of them left their footprints on the sands of time. You felt great catastrophes coming, as if the economic and political situation would necessarily get worse and precipitate Europe into the Apocalypse. You were very much unlike all the young people I knew during that time. Under your dialectician's rags, you wrote reports intended to shake us up, to move us away from the world of illusions—I mean from our world, a world which tends to ignore the notions of verisimilitude that we demand from a fable.

Ben, do you know why the dreams of children are always corrupted in the mouths of adults? Why we lose the gift of wonder and the faculty of indignation? And yet, Ben, you gave us markers, signposts, beginnings . . . Of thought, dreams and meditation. We were only a group of young Berliners eager to live. No need to respect bourgeois conventions for that. On the contrary, we had to swear and spit into the street. To live like those desert plants that have to grow in a hostile environment and need to thrust their roots deep into the soil for nourishment. To ask ourselves what really counts in the end:

enjoying the luxury of a small mansion or travelling to the Orient like Flaubert? Making a fortune from exotic wood in Gabon, or entering into a poetic trance in a garret on Rue Quincampoix, scribbling out page after page while looking lovingly at the skull wedged between the big volumes of Dante, Rabelais and Cervantes? Ah, the bohemian life!

I know you felt at home in Paris—especially at that time of your life when one associates with prostitutes, expatriates and immigrants. The city is full of them. In Paris Maurice Blanchot always had some kind words and a warm cup of coffee for you. You would sometimes meet him in a little cafe on Rue Mazarine. The two of you talked about Paris and architecture. 'Here, architecture is not just decorative,' you explained, 'it is an essential character, rooted in its history, never out of the frame, nor out of danger, nor out of the reach of cannons. No matter how hard it tries to fool us, to blend in with the landscape, to

welcome and be welcomed by the Seine,
mistress of the city. Moreover, Paris architecture makes a point of speaking the dialect
of the river's gentle meanders, of using the
patois of the four seasons, of resisting the fury
of the elements; it arches its back under the
cool of dawn and suffers under the lash of
lightning.' Blanchot would nod, his mind half
elsewhere.

You probably hide this even from yourself, Ben: you are part of that lost group,
those all too Germanized Jews who will be
able to find themselves only by going back
to the deep roots of their people and returning to the land of Israel, joining the masses
who flock from everywhere to turn the
deserts of Palestine green. Haven't you
remained that lower middle-class German
—Dr Walter Benjamin, journalist on occasion and unemployed professor, unable to
write a novel about your predicament
because you yourself are a character from a
novel? A dull life without the novelty of cool
springs or the bold adventure of ocean waves.

If you don't know who you really are, Ben, you do know where you come from and who your parents are. A traditional European family of the old school: work and education come first. There's nothing like going through your correspondence to get to know you. Admit it, Ben: you pour your whole being into your letters and travel diaries. There, your deepest self—the one you hide, erase and sometimes harass—rises to the surface.

Your fleshly self, too. Touched by the magic of the feminine continent no man can ever escape, especially if that magic is decked out in gypsy dresses, walks barefoot through the narrow streets with desire slung over its back, subtly revealing the erogenous zones. Who controls the plot of this story? You would seek a scientific explanation—or even a sensual one—for the intrinsic nature of existence. You would look for the fault-line where love takes its source. Through what detours and sorrows do we sometimes happen on that source, if we're lucky? What, then,

is the meaning of our coming into the world,
the meaning of our existence in this world,
and why must we leave it some day . . .?
(grease spots)

Azan, The Call to Prayer

Allahu akbar, Allahu akbar
Achadou an lâ ilâha illa-Allâh, Achadou an lâ ilâha
    illa-Allâh
Achadou ana Mohammadan Rasoullou-lallâh,
Achadou ana Mohammadan Rasoullou-lallâh
Hayyâ' alâ-s-salât, Hayyâ' alâ-s-salât
Hayyâ' alâ-l-falâh, Hayyâ' alâ-l-falâh,
Allahu akbar, Allahu akbar
Lâ ilâha illa-Allâh

God is most great, God is most great
I bear witness that there is no true God but Allah,
I bear witness that there is no true God but Allah,
I bear witness that Muhammad is the Messenger of
    Allah,
I bear witness that Muhammad is the Messenger of
    Allah,
Come to prayer, Come to prayer,
Come to Felicity, Come to Felicity,
God is most great, God is most great

There is no true God but Allah
There is no true God but Allah

Allahu akbar, Allahu akbar
Achadou an lâ ilâha illa-Allâh wa Achadou ana
    Mohammadan Rasoullou-lallâh
Hayyâ' alâ-s-salât
Hayyâ' alâ-l-falâh
Qad qa matiss salat
Qad qa matiss salat
Allahu akbar, Allahu akbar
Lâ ilâh illa-Allâh

God is most great, God is most great
I bear witness that there is no true God but Allah
    and Muhammad is the Messenger of Allah,
Come to prayer,
Come to Felicity,
The prayer service is ready
The prayer service is ready
God is most great, God is most great
There is no true God but Allah

II

Bab-El-Mandeb
Or The a e Tear

Bab-el-Mandeb—literally the 'gate of tears' in Arabic—is the strait that separates the Arabian peninsula from Africa and connects the Red Sea to the Gulf of Aden in the Indian Ocean. It is both an important location strategically and one of the most heavily used navigation corridors in the world.

The narrowest spot in the strait is about thirty kilometres wide, between Ras Mannali on the Yemenite coast and Ras Siyyân in Djibouti. The island of Perim divides the strait into two channels. The eastern channel, known as Bab Iskender, 'the channel of Alexander,' is three kilometres wide, with a maximum depth of thirty metres. The western channel, or Dact-el-Mayun, is twenty-five kilometres wide and three hundred and ten metres deep. A small archipelago known as the 'Seven Brothers' is located near the African coast.

According to an Arab legend, its name comes from the tears of those who were drowned by the earthquake that separated Asia from Africa. Another explanation attributes the origin of the name to the dangers of navigating the channel.

•

Secrets

I start my day with a continental breakfast, while underlining three words with a yellow marker: mobility, discretion, efficiency. That's the motto of Adorno Location Scouting, named in honour of a famous German thinker. It is also the guiding principle of my investigation. I must admit I'm a lot less efficient here than in Denver, Los Angeles or Melbourne. It's the fault of this country. I can't manage to get a handle on these people: they're too elusive. Too standoffish with me, because they know they're being watched. The fault of the past, which sometimes overcomes my will.

I just don't have what it takes to be a tough investigator. I've remained the same timid, shy, solitary boy. Rarely laughing, playing just as rarely, never managing to fill up the distance that separates me from other people. A heart harder than flint. I would always take refuge in reading and studying first

147

French, then English. I would also take refuge in day-dreaming. Grandpa Assod and his people viewed dreams as messages sent to men by higher powers, whether benevolent or diabolical. Dreams enable us to predict the near future just like the weather forecasts of our modern times. Isn't it possible to use the skills of my ancestors, who could decode the world of the night, to forge ahead in my investigation? Could I use Grandpa Assod's premonitions as a GPS?

I had reached that point in my thoughts when I was submerged by my little voice again. I could see the face of the sad child I was then, straining to learn how to read the Koran. It wasn't easy. Around me, the other children, like my little cousins Samatar and Soufiane as well as my brother Djamal, were learning at exemplary speed. Words flew from their mouths with extraordinary ease. For me, the effort of emitting a sound was insurmountable, as if my own tongue was trapped in a concrete sheath. My whole body was caught in the net of its emotions. For weeks at a time I would repeat fragments of the suras I overheard in the family courtyard without understanding their meaning. I would give up in frustration. I was overcome with shame and my belly was getting heavier and heavier as if that burden were drying up my tearless body. As if hot ashes were being poured into my throat, preventing me from uttering the slightest sound. As if, in the end, the Koranic language and death were allied against my small person. Yes, they were of the same kind: they wore the same waxen mask.

As language was fading away inside me, death took shape, and my carcass was infused with tremendous pain. I would stay on the alert, for I refused to let myself be surprised by sleep. You never know. Never let your guard down, for death is a bitch, the nastiest of traitors. I stayed up late. I talked to myself to keep my courage up. And I would begin to make out the features, angles and contours of the Grim Reaper in the thick darkness. That must be him, or was it his ghost? I could not fail to recognize him in the horde of wanderers who speak the language of men so poorly. In his eye, the suns were extinguished. No need for an interpreter of dreams to read fear, the sheer panic on my face. Move forwards, question, learn, keep learning. That was the source of everything—of this series of questions, too: 'Where do I come from, where am I, where am I going?' I was learning, with one eye aimed at the world and the other turned towards the night of the womb. Let's face it: Montreal is the place where I feel most at home. Even during my student years in Paris, I had no body, I floated in a vaporous state, and winter didn't help. Eight thousand kilometres away, my brother and his frail body were also looking for a solid support that would give them shape. I missed 'Little Brother' a lot but I had to think of myself first. I was sliding over the wet cobblestones of Paris, carried along by the crowd or forever alone.

I know now that my mother dreamed of another child, a child who would be better than I was. A perfect child, like the little sister who had died before my birth. There was no way I could fight against that ideal. From her window, she could see the sand whirling, rising towards the sky and falling back in particles of dust. She wanted a girl with hair black as mourning and the gentle features usually attributed to cherubs. My mother had other secrets, other dreams, in which I had no place. In the stories she told herself, my place was empty. In the family album, too.

Even when I was a baby crying in her arms, she would manage to pass me off to someone else: a relative, a neighbour or the maid—a young girl marked by hunger, driven from her camp by the last drought. There was no use trying to attract her attention or beg for a hug, as she would always find some way, some kind of trick, to dodge me. When we were alone together, she would take refuge in sleep or improvise an urgent prayer, the sixth or seventh that she owed the Lord and was giving back to Him on the spot. I would wait quietly for the end of her long prayer as I lay next to her on her rug with my eyes glued to the supple body of my mother folding herself together, unfolding and refolding at each unit—each *rakaat*—of the prayer. I would turn over and over again in my mouth the words I had to find to get the ghost of a smile or the shadow of a glance. She remained aloof and kept reciting her suras, only looking me in the eye at the end of her prayer. She had no gestures or words for me. For her, I was no more than a puzzle, an enigma that was slipping downwards, lower and lower.

•

Ra

Believe me if you will. One day as I faced the sea, I opened a book and my whole life was changed. I was twenty and once again I'd failed the baccalaureate, that cursed exam at the end of secondary school which opens the doors of life to you like magic. The paper took on life, becoming a mirror or a screen. From the very first words, a solemn voice welcomed you. It took you by the hand and never let you go again.

One day I opened the Koran and my whole life was changed by it. Now I know that this book never ends at the last sentence. It has nothing in common with those little invented stories that let you escape from reality and entertain you for a while. In their company, you keep turning inside the confines of illusion, you follow the meanders of madness. You get lost in Berlin with the author of your bedtime reading. It is easy to lose oneself in literature. It does bring back the princesses of former times but you learn nothing of the great mystery of life. The charm of

those paper characters is as artificial as your own life,
my false brother. I was once a voracious, compulsive
reader—a very long time ago. I have changed. It is
true that my curiosity for books has returned since
I discovered that mysterious palimpsest and the
unfortunate life of old Ben. But I blame this passing
sentimentality on my former past. I take good care of
my armour. Nothing will be as it was before, when my
mind was still free and welcomed works of imagination and reflection. Today, I am on a more reliable,
solid track. I am following in the traces of my spiritual
Guide. I am his shadow. I am the apple of his eye. I
am his wrist, his fighting arm, I read only the Divine
Book . . .

The Book of Ben

. . . the only land in which you can fully exercise your talents, Ben, is the land of freedom.
Without freedom, life, reading and writing are
impossible. Only silence and exile remain—
exile with its train of miseries and its moments
of happiness. Paris was holding its arms out
to you, and you could not ignore it for long.
It is the last European city, the last bastion

of what used to be the dominant culture. Outside Paris your emotional and sensorial universe remains dull. You used to whisper to yourself repeatedly: 'I must keep going with a high heart. Paris, I will take you on! The whole round world will open up for me. To wake men to the world—that is my task for the months to come. An old buried dream will surface again, gain strength again.' And you traded the grey dullness of a Berlin winter for the vigour of a Paris summer ...

I would like my whole life to be held between the pages of the great Divine Book. My wish will be granted, or not. I am patient, I can bide my time, for all is in the hands of Allah The Compassionate, the Ever Returning.

A Messenger

After midnight today I am no longer covered by my employer. My expenses and security will be completely my own responsibility. Of course, there is no question of running away just when I'm beginning to untangle the threads of my investigation. My mission is at a turning point. Forty-eight more hours and I'll be able to wrap-up this damned job. The last two days have not been a total waste of time for some.

The man has kept watch in front of the entrance to the hotel, protected by three huge men in green uniforms armed with Kalashnikovs—at least that's what he claims. He has known my identity for a long time. He already has some idea of how my investigation is going, he says with a smile of would-be complicity. He's been following me ever since I arrived without my noticing it. Disguised as an ordinary citizen, he had no problem tailing me.

When I saw him coming with his gigantic strides encumbered by his djellaba, I thought he was coming to get some money out of me by pretending to be a distant cousin on my great-grandmother's side. A moment later, his athletic look and his noble bearing led me to think otherwise.

Then I thought he was going to lecture me, reproach me for the way I was dressed or some other infraction. I thought he, too, had given himself the mission of bringing me back to the path traced by the Prophet Muhammad for all the men and women on this earth. Now and again, some individuals decide who should be brought back to the straight and narrow, with the idea that this way they will earn their place in Paradise. Utter nonsense. I did not want to bend my knee or bow my head.

Finally, he came right up to me and stood there, measuring me from head to foot. I was trembling slightly, wondering if Denise would have noticed how uncomfortable I was. An unknown hand has put this man on my trail, I said to myself as I observed his features. Despite his sloppy dress, you got the feeling he had the authority to be obeyed to the letter. Why this attire? Was he hiding a secret he himself knew nothing about?

Something was telling me a number of intelligence agencies kept a data sheet on this man. If it wasn't us, it would be our competitors, who worked for the petromonarchies and the finest diamond dealers. I was not mistaken: better still, I easily found his identity sheet in our data bank. His career is emblematic. After being unemployed for a long time, Abshir was recruited by the neighbourhood imam. The man has character: he cut his teeth on the allocation of humanitarian aid. In 1992, he was sent to Mogadishu, then ravaged by civil war; he distributed flour, rice and milk. Weapons in hand, he skimmed off his cut before the twenty-eight thousand cubic metres of food—dropped by the American soldiers of UNOSOM—could fall into the laps of the warlords. Then he joined one of those warlords and successfully climbed every step of this profession. He was, by turns, a low-level thug with a quick trigger, a cutthroat who turned the skin of his victim inside out like a wineskin, a hostage-taker, a bodyguard and a Red Sea pirate. He distinguished himself as a human bombshell sent out to all fields of operation. From his first baptism of fire on, he took terrible risks, but his survival instinct allowed him to get through. Whether going solo or as squad leader, the man was always extremely effective. His face shows traces of those years of hardship. If he died, he would be entitled to a special prayer. They would weave laurels for the orphan from Ali-Sabieh, who had become a valiant soldier of Al-Ittihaad al-Islaami! He would have deserved the celestial pleasures and the houris of Paradise!

The day he left to go out on jihad, the neighbourhood imam gave Abshir a white turban and a lump of earth that he always kept with him. He took part in every combat and went through all the quagmires of the region. He was seen in Ogaden, in the outskirts of Mombasa, the maquis of Puntland, the djebels of Yemen, in Kandahar, and in the Sudanese militias. He wore a beard dyed with henna, a Palestinian keffiyeh, and the Pakistani salwar kameez. He escorted precious containers (weapons, telephone equipment) from the Djibouti terminal to the zone where the borders of Ethiopia, Somalia and Kenya meet. He guided and protected envoys, enabling them to travel through whole areas without paying ransoms either to the regular troops who charge multiple traffic tolls, or to warlords of many allegiances. He disappeared for a few months and then reappeared. He was seen on *The Arsenal of the Faith*, the TV show of Ibtisam Sheikh

Youssouf, the muse of reformed artists who have deserted the stage for the rigorous practice of Islam. After that, he headed the personal guards of Mursal Hadji Yacine, a tele-Koranist who defines himself as a diamond visible to God alone. Once again he vanished from sight. Unfounded rumours had him on the Island of Socotra, where unspeakable plots were being hatched. Then he came back to Djibouti.

In short, Abshir is a tiny but precious cog in the machinery that is meant to defend the Dar al-Islam, or Community of the Faithful, against the assaults of the Crusaders. This knight of the Faith showed great qualities of analysis and endurance on every field of operation.

Although he is illiterate, Abshir came up with maxims which could energize regiments of combatants and throw adolescents from the Dutch, British or Swedish slums into the skirmishes to defend their brothers humiliated or massacred in Ramallah, Kosovo or Bosnia. At the age of thirty-three, he is a very experienced man, who was able to train dozens of combatants and lead and then dissolve a military cell in a few weeks.

The time has come for him to take another direction, to disappear from the screens. To change identity, to distance himself from the organization. Even if he doesn't admit it to himself, the man has doubts about the justness of the cause to which he gave the best years of his life. Weary of the infighting, he chose to bury himself in an oasis and keep out of sight before coming back and settling in a nearby town. He came to see me, he says, of his own volition. He gave me a few precious bits of information in exchange for a small fortune. I would have done the same thing if I were in his shoes. He opened my eyes to the career of my own brother Djamal, who must be hiding somewhere or rotting in prison as a follower of the great ideologue.

From one day to the next, Abshir will cease to exist. He will vanish from the screens. Another combatant will take his place. His name will be Kassim, Amir, Bourhan-Eddin, Khalif al-Suri, Farouk Alakusoglu or Hafiz the Bengali. Risks weighed and accepted. He will be just as effective. And, of course, they do not know each other.

●

Zay

I am an early convert to the mujahideen, a resistance fighter in the service of The Compassionate full of compassion! Through His grace, I was put under the high protection of His Eminence, my Guide on this earth. Since then I have been his shadow, his goose quill and his two eyes, sharp as an eagle's. I have been sentenced to death like him. I am the lieutenant of the terrorist organization The New Way, as they say in their administrative jargon. There are thirty charges against us. Terrorist attacks, targeted assassinations, undermining national sovereignty, intelligence with the Taliban, incitement to uprising, arms trafficking, introduction of the green uniform and black mask of the Islamist militias, forbidding the use of khat and so on. We are accused of every conceivable crime.

I will see my Master through to the end, if only to defy the authorities of this world. My fate is linked to that of my venerable Sayid, all the more so as our head of operations is no longer active in the field. He must have withdrawn to let the storm pass. Those infidels at the head of the State are unaware that only The Sovereign has the right of life and death over us poor slaves. And we are many, both inside the jails and out. Very many. The mujahideen brothers and sisters, sons and daughters of the twelve cities blessed in times past, are all here at our sides, ready to give up what is most dear to them. Ready to put on the immaculate turban of the martyrs or more exactly of the shahids. Ready to welcome their brothers and comrades in arms from the four corners of the earth. Ready to make a video of their last will and testament before throwing this country into the purifying fire.

Just listen to their testimony, censored by the government press. It happened right near here a few hours after the latest attack. Yes, you can transcribe them and send them off to the news agencies and your sponsors.

'As-salaam Aleikum! Ah, it's you, Fazul the Cormorian! They're looking for you everywhere, they say. The Americans and their lackeys have put a price on your head. Your face is posted everywhere. Oh, the despicable wretches! Do they not know that only Allah the Helper has the power to call you to His side?'

'*Ahlan*! My name is Abdousamad Darwish. I have no nationality now. I am a Muslim combatant, and that is all. Only yesterday, the Crusaders and the sons of Judah fled before our missiles.'

'And you, Ahmet Hamza, child of Asmara, they say you joined the struggle from the very first days! *Wa Allahu Alem*! Your reputation has crossed the borders of Eritrea. Come in, my brother, take this cushion.'

'I was the lieutenant of Djokar the Chechen. I headed the group of brothers who put to flight the Abyssinian army paid by Washington. We drove them out of Mogadishu and Baidhabo with the help of The Most Honorable. Ogaden will soon be free. Allahu akbar!'

'May the martyrs rest in peace! And may their exemplary actions stir up more brothers!'

'Full of radiance, they have gone to Paradise!'

'Amin.'

There is not just one kind of resistance fighter, as the government press keeps repeating. Don't forget, you sand snake, we know everything because everything is reported back to us here. The resistance has a thousand faces, as the night has a thousand and one stars. Its birth was spontaneous, but its victory took a long time to take shape. True, at the start there was improvisation, even discord among our combatants. Fire was smoldering in our ranks, and it took us three full years to purge our troops of dubious elements—the eunuchs, the weak and the Judases. Allah the Avenger could not abandon us in this pitiful state, stuck as we were between the stones of the desert and the cannons of our enemies.

A man arose, called by destiny, and he said what had to be said. He took the head of a little group that had almost been decimated by the bullets of the prevaricators. He gathered a handful of men around him. He made pacts with other groups on the brink of discouragement. He tightened our lines, mended connections, laid down rules of hygiene and gave clear instructions. A courageous man, he won his first victories sword in hand. Then he multiplied ambushes, skirmishes and sabotage. He made frontal attacks in broad daylight. With those mujahideen of a new kind, the prevaricators no longer knew what strategy to adopt. Inspired by Satan, they opted for the worst of all tactics. With a great deal of money, they were able to hire impious soldiers and sign pacts with foreign powers that are nothing more than the military branch of the Vatican or Israel. The cowards showed their true face to the Community of Believers. That was a turning point. Fresh recruits came pouring in, and not just disoriented young men, as it has often been said. But also battalions of mature men who had seen the light, fathers encouraged by their imam, and even a few robust old men. All were aware that it was the start of a new era, and they wanted to play a role in it. They wanted to leave the *Jahiliyyah* to go back to earlier times, in the footsteps of our Fragrant Prophet Muhammad—may His name be praised forever!— and of His Companions.

The Book of Ben

. . . would that little path lined with olive trees really be your final home? In any case, that's what I would have chosen for my eternal rest if I were hunted by the Gestapo, as you were. During the years of exile, there could have been other homes, other retreats for you, Ben. When I think about it, I could picture you just as easily buried in an Andalusian village baking under the hot sun; in a dried-out riverbed in Arizona; or in a hamlet haunted by the African gods in the heart of Guadeloupe. Every time I see you in my dreams, now that you've been lucky enough to leave that internment camp, my heart flies to the little path lined with olive trees. I can't help it. When you lie on this earth, you will appreciate—as I do—the storms and torrents that flattened the bed of the wadi all the way to my African prison. For me, it is quite obvious: this is where I will die. The rocky earth will receive me. I will have a little green hole just big enough for me in the middle of this ocean of stones. The days and the nights will pursue their eternal rounds. It is said that when you are born, the spirit gets to meet its envelope. When you die, it is united with the earth . . .

●

Revolt in the Desert

Abshir, Djamal, Abdelaziz al-Afghani or Mohammed ibn Albani, the name is of no importance. One must face facts: it is always the same pawn at work, controlled from a distance by faceless groups, somewhat like hidden multinational corporations. But where is the fire coming from? Who gains from it? These are legitimate questions. They are, however, beyond the scope of my investigation.

Extremely ancient, underground links run from one corner of the planet to another. It is up to us, the foot soldiers of intelligence, to connect the scattered threads and bring the whole fabric to light. The sceptic only sees the surface of things. Whether frightened or indignant, he goes from surprise to surprise. I was stupefied to learn that an insurrection took place in the very heart of the international complex in Dubai. Was it a planned action or a spontaneous fit of rage? We shall soon know the answer. Meanwhile, one question is on everyone's mind: Who are those men who rise up and then escape from that camp in the middle of nowhere? Those men who take a prisoner with them, give him handfuls of rice with oil to fatten him up, and when the day comes, cut their ounce of flesh from him to escape death, always on the prowl. Who are they? The pariahs of the Persian Gulf—that's what the press has called them after an incisive story in *Newsweek*—make up the dark side of our glittering capitalism. Millions of people from India, Bangladesh, Sri Lanka, the Horn of Africa or the Philippines are building, with all their strength and sweat, the futuristic high-rises that make Riyadh, Bahrain and Dubai the avant-garde of the kitsch world. A few days ago, those men buried in the depths of the endless winter of modern slavery rebelled against the working conditions their construction boss imposed on them. They killed him: they're no longer risking deportation, but death. They had to take flight. Soon they will join other men gathered in the desert. Galvanized, whipped up by sermons, dressed in white, they will rush off to attack the vertical towers, the palaces of mirrors and the artificial islands that vainly and endlessly try to imitate the golden age of a vanished Andalusia.

These are not just rumours any more. Our services have confirmed that these men in long white tunics are already there. They are operational, or at least most of them are. Quantity isn't what counts in this kind of decision. They are here because in Dubai, Tangiers or Djibouti, the goal is the same: to cut out the heart of this corrupt world, destroy its foundations, throw them into the flames and hasten the advent of a healthier, more sober world, entirely ruled by the Supreme Book. They keep saying that this world they seek is not an illusion or a short-lived utopia. It is a world that once existed, and devoted all its energy to worshipping Allah and Him alone! Faxes sent out to various editorial offices trumpet the message: By the will of Allah—praise be to The Most Lofty—this blessed world will return. These men are just waiting for the signal. Hence the urgency of my investigation, too. Of course, I couldn't stop this plot all by myself. I am only a small pawn in a vast enterprise with global ramifications connecting zones of poverty and oases of abundance, authentic believers and out-and-out criminals. It starts from the Horn, branches out into the heart of Africa, comes back through maritime routes, western banks, North

American bureaus, plunges into the Urals and the petromonarchies of the Gulf before ending its journey in various offshore tax havens.

I did well not to get discouraged. My first informer put me on the trail of the mysterious Frenchwoman. Abshir's testimony revealed to me how very long ago that project of destabilization had begun. I have to deal with the psychology of the locals, marked by fear and rumour. They cultivate fear and rumour on both sides of the Red Sea the way others cultivate yams or poppies. For the first time since I got here, I have some reason to be pleased with myself.

Well done, Djib! Bravo! I encouraged myself.

●

Sin

O you the charlatan of my insomnias, listen to what follows!

We trained young people who had never been heard in this region before, superior listeners, readers unspoiled by any parental—or worse still, foreign— contamination. They are sincere: they go to the very roots of words, they fight to conquer the space the Sacred Letter lost in the darkness of corrupted regimes that practice lying and hypocrisy, from Algiers to Jakarta.

We began to hunt down printed matter, books of fiction intended to erode our memory, stories that deride the very foundations of our traditions. Do not smile, my friend, for we know that these works—newspapers and books of poetry—did not come to our land on their own. They are agents of contamination, the tin soldiers of an impious order. I'm well aware, though, that all this has not disarmed our enemy. The Christian West and its Jewish manoeuverers will stop at nothing. They succeeded in subduing us because they first succeeded in dividing us into different groups, tribes and clans. Better still, they found traitors in our ranks. But we have already begun to foil their diabolical plan.

From now on, our salvation is our faith. And our faith makes us strong. We want nothing to do with people who are stimulated by mischief and laughter. We must get used to their non-existence even if they are still in this world. Our children will not leave them a drop of breathable air if we keep up our momentum, with the help of the Most Gracious. Our victory will be complete; it is only a matter of months now. You can write it down in black and white and proclaim it to the whole world! We will come to enjoy the milk and myrrh of Paradise.

Already our enemies are panic-stricken and scattering to the four corners of the globe. We have learned that the sultans of Assab and Obock have taken refuge in foreign embassies. Others were luckier and found a closet the size of their honour in western capitals. We have promised the New Way. We will achieve the New Way, with the assistance of The Immutable.

Stay ready, soldiers of Allah! Sharpen your sight, listen at doors, spy on what takes place in the intimacy of bedrooms. The first signals carried by the horde of combatants will reach you easily. As for the rest, we must have patience, as our Holy Prophet demands. We will succeed in dissolving our enemies as salt dissolves ice.

'May I confess something to you?' murmurs my venerable Master as he turns to me. 'Swear before The Compassionate full of compassion that for now you will keep it locked in the safe of your heart.'

Decidedly, his trust in me has limits which I find offensive.

He pursues his diatribe. 'The precepts of our pro-gramme were set down, he says softly, on silk paper, gathered in a luxurious volume, with illuminations glorifying the divine radiance. In the near future you will hold this book in your hands and show it to the other brethren, God willing! I have said all I have to say to you. The time of jihad has come. Tell our combat-ants outside to arise. Give the signal. Tell them this:

' "Go forth, with your sabers raised high. You are pioneers, valiant and precious. We will drive out the infidels and their lackeys. Our ranks are constantly swelling; reinforcements are coming from afar. From the depths of the equatorial forest—from Rwanda, Congo and Angola, ordinary people are converting en masse and following in the footsteps of the Salafs, our pious predecessors, may God bless them! Nothing can resist our words of awakening. With the aid of The Utterly Just, we will build one unified Islamic State throughout the Horn of Africa. It is only a question of time now . . ."'

And now my pen is bumping up against the other writing. Is it due to chance? I have no idea . . .

The Book of Ben

. . . more than anything, you love pasting pieces together when you tell stories, Ben. Piling stories on top of each other like the palimpsests of medieval times. Organization and classification are tempting but they do not suit your stories. You will leave traces in people's memories. Perhaps one day, through luck or a miracle, the narrative of your life will be resuscitated. Perhaps some witness, as far away as I am now, will set your unfortunate life down on paper. Then the task will be to tell the bits and pieces of your existence. You, Walter Benjamin, fleeing the Germanic order of the Third Reich, leaving Paris much against your will. So I've been calling you Ben without knowing why for as long as I can remember. For a long time, I wondered who had the absurd idea of giving a first name as silly as Walter to a highly assimilated bourgeois Jew. I will keep on calling you Ben for the sake of convenience. I will unwind the thread of your messianic life in the course of the next few days if I have any paper left. I had the whimsical idea of decorating the whole thing with little drawings, scribbles and ink blots. Everyone knows you used to collect rare old books, precious works and incunabula with or without illuminations. I am trying to illuminate my little notebook in my own way with the means at hand.

And by conversing with you like this, I am also trying to set my own story straight— a story that ends in this jail at the end of the world. By these returns to the past, I emerge from an interminable sleep that I cannot quite manage to escape. I must hurry, for no one knows when the abyss will swallow me up, nor where and when it will cough me up again. Perhaps in the heart of this prison collapsing with the passage of time. A prison made entirely of basalt rocks surrounded by a bamboo fence.

Everything here is stone. People around here are born with the knowledge of stone engrained in their bodies. Stones store heat and possess secret powers of healing. Flat, polished stones for the relief of rheumatism, grains of sand for stomach aches. Clay for pregnant women and skin care. Small pebbles meticulously arranged for blocking off evil spells. Rock, which protects against lightning. Stone flakes, a miraculous remedy prized by asthmatics. Rock formations celebrating the gods. Monoliths, steles, and tombs for opening the path to eternity. Everything here is stone.

Ah, I must not forget the present. For the moment, my present is confined to raising hares. 'Raising' them is a big word for

●

these little creatures who come and go as
they will. They rub up against the wall of
my cell, which threatens to collapse at any
moment. In this ruined world molded by
darkness, these animals stimulate me; they
are my horizon. Hares are patient animals; I
do all I can to imitate them . . .

Strange, that narrator locked in a cell, too. His
fate seems similar to mine in every way, on the threshold of certain death, like me. Yet everything separates
us, and I am not sorry for him in the slightest.

The Egg of Experience

I had absolutely no difficulty in getting the French-woman to talk. She was open to all my questions. They say truth bursts out progressively, as bubbles of oxygen rise slowly from the mud of consciousness. I walked up to her and immediately felt warm vibrations emanating from her. The iris of her eyes was a very light-brown colour that turned hazel with the light. There was a remnant of lipstick on her lips. She would nod her head and think at length, taking her time as if my words were reaching her through some other channel than the ear. Then she would answer, still taking her time. Her story was not unusual, she said. But that apparent modesty was hiding something else that had nothing to do with secrecy, but everything to do with conditioning. She couldn't wait to confide in someone. All I had to do was transcribe her testimony in my brand-new fourth notebook. We were in a courtyard rented for the occasion by my informers, in the shade of the oleanders.

A little bird told me I had to let the Frenchwoman converted to Islam talk. I listened to her unwinding the tortuous tale of her life, in Paris as well as in Djibouti and the region of Tadjoura. It wasn't that hard for her to give me the name of her saviour—the man who invited her to get a plane ticket for the Horn of Africa, welcomed her, and helped her along her way as a novice.

Ever since he had her swear on the Holy Koran, she had become a totally different person, she confided, with a shy smile.

Who is that mysterious man who had melted the heart of this woman? Why had chance put her on my path? I should be content with this result. The informers had been generously remunerated by us and had done their job. They informed on the Frenchwoman. And she in turn fingered the man who was supposed to have saved her skin.

Yet something bothers me: Why such a rush? I must not rejoice too quickly. But I must admit I find the case of these foreign women indoctrinated by criminal groups interesting, because they turn out to be more stubborn than the men, and because their self-sacrifice can go very far. At least that's what our psychologist in Adorno Location Scouting used to tell us.

•

Shin

So, you crab, the goal's in sight. Would you have the guts to come all the way out here, share our fate just for a few minutes, and get a taste of the pleasures of a cell? Oh, no, I was forgetting that generosity is not your strong point. And I hear you're calling yourself Djib. How preposterous! Are you so ashamed of your real name? Djibril. An homage to the angel Djibril, the Messenger of God. You can't possibly commit such an affront and stay alive.

How can we know everything we know about you, we who are prisoners at the periphery of the world? Don't bother your little head about it. You don't have much longer to live. First of all, you should realize that the very notion of periphery is illusory in this world where everything is connected and depends on the word of God. 'Periphery' is a serious illusion. Wherever you may be, as far as you may wander, the place you're in is the centre of the world.

We know everything about you and from this penitentiary transformed into a fortress, we act. I would come meet you and clarify things if I felt like it. And to think I was your brother in the past! To think I shared the same home with you for a good seventeen years! To think we both came out of the same womb twenty minutes apart, you and me: I'm still amazed at how different we are. Thank heaven our paths separated soon enough. You're just a cork swept away by a river, a twig adrift on the surface of things. You don't even know what you're doing. And you think your cameras, your job as a mercenary and small-time computer pirate will open the road of success for you? You're making a big mistake there, brother!

In another life I would have dreamed of writing patriotic poems and newspaper stories on current events in the Horn of Africa in order to open your eyes. Today, nothing of the sort. Fortunately, Providence decided otherwise: for five long years I strove to perfect my theological education and took care to give no sign of life, to write nothing but the sermons of my venerable Master. To tell the truth, I had never been able to find a job in this rotten country. Nothing to make ends meet. Nothing that could give me the illusion of being economically independent. They expelled me for insubordination in my second year of school. The principal there acted like a lawless little boss who lured fifteen-year-old girls into his bed—something you must have repressed since you were focusing so hard on your beloved studies. I prepared for the baccalaureate on my own, took it as an independent candidate, and failed the exam twice. I never had the slightest word of encouragement from you, or at least I don't remember any.

You left without saying a word to anybody. Neither to your parents, who were weakened by the illness that would carry them off two years later, nor to me. I went wild, and committed multiple petty thefts; I was desperate, but Allah The Generous has an inexhaustible stock of consolations to soothe our pains and frustrations. I gained the respect of those around me and my *zebiba*, that black spot on the forehead, by genuflecting, praying to The All Encompassing. I rose through the ranks to become the scribe of my venerable Master. I know many people who no longer expect anything from this world. That's all it takes to start breaking locks. An easy step to take in these times when people are starved for hope.

O you, the infidel of my childhood nightmares, I have the pleasure of informing you that the young man who is to cut your throat as he would a lamb's is ready. He is merely waiting for a sign from my venerable and pious Master. A little wave of his hand and our martyr will do his job, at the risk of his life if necessary. I will do nothing to stop the machine, quite to the contrary. When you left fifteen years ago, abandoning your family—a family, moreover, that was sorely in need—with no regret and no remorse, you signed that fatal decree yourself. I will be relieved when you are no longer in the land of the living, I will no longer have to seek your shadow at my side as I sometimes still do in my moments of weakness or my nightmares.

I'll have you know that the young man who is to cut your throat is in an excellent frame of mind. He just got married, at one of those mass weddings which the two or three richest men in the country organized at the Hotel Sheraton, precisely where you're staying. Some thirty couples were offered a free ceremony, complete with blessing, prayer, music, two slices of cake and two gold-plated wedding rings. Needless to say, we condemn these falsely charitable weddings. Everybody knows they're a subterfuge to give oneself an easy conscience. A clever way of escaping the wrath of the most extreme among us. But we couldn't refuse our valiant martyr those moments of joyous celebration. He is ready to carry out his mission. He has already recorded his will on a DVD, accompanied by the suras and verses in honour of the Chosen Ones, our martyrs Al-Shabab Almujahideen . . .

The Book of Ben

. . . That night you slept outside in a clearing, Ben. And very badly. You were lucky enough to escape from the internment camp where we lived together for three weeks. There were many foreign Jews there, German dissidents, communists from the French Resistance, and even a few gypsies. We felt sorry for you the minute we saw you. You were at the end of your rope. But a miracle happened. In a few weeks, you regained some of your energy. But you remained taciturn. Was it in Marseille that you left Siegfried Kracauer, your Frankfurter friend?

You were stammering even more than usual,
sensing the Nazi pack right on your heels. It
must have been at the end of March or the
beginning of April 1940. And a little later, in
Lourdes, you definitively lost track of your
sister Dora. Whose fault was that? You had
daydreamed long enough in Paris, in the little garrets, the noisy cafes and the den of the
Bibliothèque nationale on Rue de Richelieu.
There was not a minute to lose. You have to
leave now. You're right not to look in the
rear-view mirror, there's no point stirring up
your sorrows, you have to move forwards.
Tempt the Devil . . .

Yes, I must move forwards. It's not easy when
your feet are bound by a ball and chain, in the company of a crippled, unctuous old man. Djib, too, will
no longer be able to move forwards. And I won't have
the chance—or the heart—to see him again. It's better that way.

●

The Scent of the Mother

If all goes well, today will be the last day of my investigation. I tossed and turned in my sheets all night. Now that I have to leave, I don't feel well at all. A pain in the lower abdomen, like an animal squeezing me. Could this be a last signal from my ancestors? From the most important one, Grandpa Assod? I was eight when he died. I was roughly propelled into the adult world. I immediately cut the umbilical cord that connected me to 'Little Brother'. I became a loner, a contemplative boy. Only David found the right words to console me:

'I'm going to tell you something. You mustn't tell anyone. Not even your parents. Don't tell anyone, OK? Your grandfather isn't dead. He's with my own grandparents up above. They'll be with us everywhere we go if you think of them very hard. You mustn't tell anyone. Not anyone. Got it? It's our secret!'

David had straightened things out for me. I never doubted that my grandfather was present at my sides.

I regained my smile. Unknown to the world, we were conspiring again. We would run all over, our two hands linked together like lovers you see in films.

I know memories change the reality from which they spring but I don't think I'm wrong to imagine that David and Grandpa Assod were actually one and the same. Or more exactly that David's crystalline voice progressively covered up the cavernous voice of my grandfather. Their legacy is the most precious thing I have, and I wouldn't give it up for anything in the world. Their faces, their smells and their words will remain in my memory even when old age tolls the bell for me.

Deep inside me, I feel that I'm not going to sneak away like a little thief: I'm not going to get off so easy. Homeland, family, the past—it all sticks to you like putty and never lets go of you. I know I'm not going to get out of this hornet's nest so lightly. Something unexpected is bound to happen, but what?

After my grandfather's death, I had to face David's disappearance. As a child, I did not understand the treason of my best friend, who was at the time dearer to me than my own brother. It is only very recently that I was able to lift a corner of the veil. By burying myself in books and secret reports, I discovered the history of his community in our country and the reasons for its presence here.

August 1949. On the other bank of the Red Sea, thirty-five thousand Yemeni Jews are piled into a camp designed for three thousand. The last Jews abandon Yemen and the Arabian Peninsula after two thousand years of cohabitation with Muslims. Direction: Israel. The press of the time declares that they are the targets of a Koranic decree, and the peninsula must no longer be sullied by their presence. Rumors swell and tempers flare. In Djibouti, the tiny Israelite community, also of Yemeni origin, follows on the heels of its brethren, selling off their meagre possessions, liquidating their dark little shops at rock-bottom prices for the benefit of the big local Arab merchants who got rich as a result of this exodus.

I only learned the day before yesterday that my friend David came from this tiny community, two hundred members strong, now vanished. David is the French version of his grandfather's first name: Dawoud Yosef, buried in Jerusalem. Last name:

David. First name: Ilan. Born 27 May 1971 in Djibouti. Mother: Françoise David, hairdresser, residing 42 bis Rue de Rome. My best friend's mother was born in Israel but went to France for the love of a Frenchman; and later to Djibouti, doubtless unable, like me, to resist the call of the country, the land of her ancestors. David was born here. The carbon copy of the birth certificate I unearthed in City Hall does not mention his father's identity, but he must have come forward one day and sent my friend a plane ticket to Paris. When I left Djibouti in 1979, I am sure that he himself knew nothing of the history of the Yemenite Jews in the country of his childhood. How his ancestors got here, why they all left at the same time, and also why their synagogue was burnt to the ground after their departure. And as for me, I wonder why we called our childhood friend by his last name and not his first. Who knows?

The fog of the past has covered up the landscapes of my childhood. Life did the rest. David left. I haven't seen my brother again since I was eighteen. I suppose that ever since he was a little child, he, too, was looking for a bit of attention or even a glance that would give him the feeling he existed. That's what I would guess, but in truth I have no idea. I never heard from him. I'm making hypotheses here, reconstructing his path in life with the little pieces of information I was able to gather later on. At the age of nineteen or twenty, my brother joined the community of other men who were fascinated by the direction the Egyptian fanatics had taken. Those men had found refuge in caves in Upper Egypt. A religious movement was born there, it seems, and then scattered out over the world. Founded in 1971 by Mustafa Shukri, an Egyptian agronomist, hardened in the jails of his country. Its name is 'Anathema and Exile' or Takfir wal Hijra. Its doctrine: a complete break with the Muslim society it called 'infidel'. Its goal: to regain the purity of the first Muslims by any means possible. The movement would continue to prosper on the ruins of Egyptian society and its mentor would continue to hasten the day of the resurrection of the dead. My brother had other masters who venerated the exemplary path traced by Mustafa al-Shukri. He was in touch with groups like the one led by the famous Ramadan al-Turki, which operated in South Yemen and in the Muslim community of Kenya, but none was more violent and radical than Takfir wal Hijra.

My brother changed guides, turbans and fronts a number of times. I was able to follow his peregrinations to some extent by cross-checking the notes from intelligence agencies and theological forums which invaded the Internet early on. With the companions who were with him from the start, they propagate their teachings, revealing the epic story of the first believers, which had long remained hidden afterwards, according to them. That's how my brother came to follow other groups too, of which I know nothing, and returned two or three years earlier to the land of his birth, the land that could not keep him.

●

Sad

I wouldn't like to be in your shoes when you cross the path of our valiant martyr. Apparently, in the beginning we are afraid to die, then after a certain stage, we are afraid not to be able to die immediately. Afraid of the agonies of death. That is what my venerable Master teaches and he's an expert on the subject, for he trained a legion of martyrs. As he has been behind bars for decades, he is no longer as active as he was at the time he went around the djebels, the maquis and the caves, like the valiant Emir Ibn Saud, but he hasn't forgotten everything either. Ever since a grenade robbed him of his sight, he sees the world through a blood-coloured film. Serenely, he turned down the offer of freedom extended by the authorities who have never broken off contact with our HQ in Doha. Twice, he rejected the offers they made him on the feast day of Eid ul-Fitr. 'Kill me if you like,' he declared, immediately adding that all power is in the hands of Allah alone—not in the hands of your little tyrant!

I confess that all this wearies me. I must admit I am not as motivated as I was before. My Master is unctuous and terribly manipulative. I wonder if deep down, I don't hate this old man and miss my freedom. I used to be young, poor, wild with anger and frustration, but at least I was free. Free to come and go, free to smoke a cigarette or chew khat with my neighbourhood friends. Free to call out to girls on the street or flirt with them. It's true that I didn't have a penny in my pocket to take them out for a drink but at least I could tease them a little.

It is useless to regret the past. All is in the hands of The Architect. Everything that happens to us is a test that He ordered. I am a motionless traveller now; I spend hours watching my Master's face which is drier than a wadi without a shower of rain, calmer than an oasis. Every time he breathes, his chest and the whole upper part of his body rise and then crash down again like waves on rocks. I live to the rhythm of that swell. The health of my estimable Master is precarious. It is no more than a cork tossed about by the waves.

As I watch him for hours on end, I find in this exercise an intense concentration which verges on trance. We are connected to each other through the swaying of his lungs. Day and night, we are the beating of the sea. We are the silence of the stone. I pray alone, keeping my distance from my Master. But I increasingly listen with half an ear, more and more distractedly, to his commentaries, missives, monologues and disputes with other *ulemas* about this or that verse, this or that part of the Hadith. When I'm not lovingly tending to my scroll of loose pages, I occasionally drift off into daydreams, and I have sinful thoughts. After all, I am only a humble human being, a mere worm compared to my Guide. I dream of women's bodies. I hunger for caresses. I thirst for kisses. I sigh and groan in orgasm. Satan has set his heart on me. All I can do now is think of the soap that washes away sin. As for Satan, he urges me to go on with my guilty activities and sinful thoughts. For I often dream of long diaphanous sprays released on fleshy thighs. I dream of flesh—caressed, possessed, loved and quickly abandoned. I dream of grape-red nipples, supple buttocks, smooth vaginas, open vulvas. I am wholly concentrated on my solitary pleasure.

My rage is increasing tenfold. It found you, or more exactly, you came to find it, all by yourself. You

should not have put yourself in my path. You should-
n't have abandoned your family like a coward, as you
did fifteen years ago. You shouldn't have come back
to the scene of your crime to mock the memory of
your parents. You shouldn't have stirred up the ghosts
of the past, my ex-brother. Above all, you should not
have worked for those people. My revenge will not go
unaccomplished.

The Book of Ben

. . . yes, it was cold in the mountains on that
day of 25 September 1940. You were shivering because you didn't have any warm
clothes. Just your worn-out jacket, a not very
clean white shirt, dark-grey trousers and
shoes well beyond repair. In the afternoon
you had all left to climb the mountain for an
inspection. Your companions will go back
down to Banyuls-sur-Mer and come back up
again at dawn. Not you, you don't have the
strength. They leave you alone on the moun-
tainside. 'It's just for an hour, there's no danger,' you whispered, as much to reassure
them as to buck yourself up. You slip under

the blanket given to you by Micheline Azéma, the wife of the Mayor of Banyuls-sur-Mer, with your precious briefcase for a pillow. Sleep is slow in coming. You count the stars, and you watch the film of your life again and again. At the first gleam of dawn, your fellow travellers come back to get you on the chilly plateau. The forest is still asleep in the mist and the dew of the night.

You don't seem well, but you are moved nonetheless by some subterranean energy. The energy of despair, of a snake trying to put as much distance as possible between itself and its dead skin. You start out at dawn. You trot along behind the trio. Each step rips out a piece of your heart. You're panting like a workhorse that has collapsed under the weight of a loaded cart. Your companions, who would have gone quickly down the side of the mountain, rein in their eagerness. They have to stop for you every thirty metres or so. And your legs start to wobble, Ben, as if they wanted to do away with the atavistic reflex of walking, as if their motion was being curbed by an unknown force. You tell yourself that you have to keep walking; after all, men have been crawling over this earth forever, like caterpillars waiting for the diaphanous butterfly they bear within. All of you are concentrated, serious, hunching up your shoulders as day breaks over Catalonia.

And in the port of Lisbon, your second destination if all goes well, they're already selling their catch. The cries of the fishmongers mingle with the noise of the garbage trucks. Newspapers are airing the big stories of the day which will become obsolete overnight. The people of Lisbon sink into muddled certainties and go to bed at ten, leaving the ghost of Fernando Pessoa whirling like a dervish from hill to hill. Perhaps luck will lead you to the port of Lisbon and beyond, to New York. The efforts of your friends Max Horkheimer, Theodor and Gretel Adorno and, of course, Hannah Arendt, all settled in the new Mecca, will not be in vain. When good fortune really wants to smile, nothing can resist it.

Now you only need to go through that little corridor for smugglers, the Lister Pass and its vault of fog. You only have to present your documents to Spanish Customs in Portbou. They're certainly no more inhuman than the hulking watchdogs of the Gestapo or the dark muzzles of Vichy. Afterwards, nothing will be the way it was before. The great American plains have always been able to feed the cohorts of poor beggars from the four corners of Europe; why should they refuse to offer their nourishing breast to a shy, refined philosopher, an old-fashioned humanist who has his Proust, his Baudelaire and Kant at his fingertips?

At every step, Ben, you have the distinct feeling that you're tottering. And the whole world seems to be toppling over with you. You stop, you massage your chest and, most often, you try to catch your breath for a few long minutes. The little band—Lisa Fittko, a friend from Berlin, and Henny Gurland with her son José, whom you met on the way— imitates you. They leave you—a plump little hunch-backed man—the time to collect yourself again. You say nothing. You keep your dignity. A dirty grey rain has been pursuing you, or at least that's what you think as you measure the distance you've covered, with your hand cupped over your forehead. Behind you, far below, the village of Banyuls-sur-Mer is waking up under the drizzle. It is autumn, and the Pyrenees are sinking into the melancholy of a dawn streaked with sea-winds. You must pick up your step, and that's what you do without even looking back.

I will not shed a tear over the body of my brother; but I will not let myself be carried away by the unctuous voice of my Master. I still have these scattered pages. I hang on to them tightly; I have become attached to these bits of dog-eared paper. I start at the slightest distant noise that reaches this cursed cell, like the old philosopher on his path over the ridge. Already I am wandering. I think I'm losing my mind.

To See 'Little Brother' Again

Denise must be fast asleep at this time; it's still night over there. May she sleep in peace! She gave me everything. I am her little man. I spent beautiful days in her company, with a book by Walter Benjamin within easy reach or the music of Abdullah Ibrahim in my ears. A pianist of that stature does not play for us mere humans. No, he plays for archangels and seraphim. His calls to prayer stir up a breath of fresh air surging from the deepest part of the cosmos, rivaling the prayers of John Coltrane in *A Love Supreme*, recorded in 1965—seven years before John Lennon's song 'Power to the People' and twelve years before my birth.

The same enchantment, the same demand for love and the absolute, can be found in the early writings of Walter Benjamin. To read a page of his *Berlin Childhood* and listen to Abdullah Ibrahim's whispers with one ear is an experience to be renewed every time one goes through a difficult patch in life.

●

Born in Cape town in 1934, classified as 'mixed-race' according to the laws of apartheid, that artist gave up his real family name, Adolph Johannes Brand, after his conversion to Islam in 1968. He will be Abdullah. Servant of Allah. By turns a pianist and singer, soprano saxophonist, flutist, cellist and singer, he always works wonders. Yet nothing predestined him to rise so high and become that virtuoso Sufi.

If Denise saved my life, Abdullah Ibrahim showed me the way. It's true that I haven't become as pious as him but the spiritual dimension of life no longer frightens me. An empty, freezing universe without God does not appeal to me. A universe made only of magnetic fields and mineral dust whirling aimlessly around on itself? No thanks. I prefer the airy, intertwined sounds and silences of Abdullah Ibrahim. To each his own way, to each his music and his destiny. I even understand my brother's tragic path somewhat better. He had nothing to lose. He was already lost, crumbling away inside, like me when I lost our mother's affection. He frantically looked everywhere for eyes which would mirror his own.

What would I do tomorrow if I found myself facing my brother here, in this very courtyard, where I'm writing up the testimony of the Frenchwoman converted to Islam under the guidance of that man Aref? Would I have the courage to take him in my arms? To wipe out the vagaries of the past by a wave of a magic wand? I ask myself these questions, I have doubts, and yet I show nothing on the outside and continue to plumb the mysterious connections between the Frenchwoman and her confessor Aref.

I prick up my ears, nervously, my senses on the alert. Every noise rips a piece out of my heart. Are the two guardian angels I took with me watching outside? Are they there to protect me or betray me? To eliminate me, perhaps, and then steal everything I have? Children are still playing in the alley across the street. No suspicious sound for the moment. No sign that could justify the panic burning inside me.

●

Dhad

Since you came back to Djibouti, lured by the bait of money, since you deliberately chose your camp—the side of the Judeo-Crusaders—your fate has surely been sealed by now.

Qays got the green light from us last night. He fully accepted his mission. He was calm, absent from this world. Don't worry, Djibril, you won't feel a thing. You won't even feel the blade of the dagger that will cut your throat because you never felt anything in your life. I don't envy you, false brother, I feel sorry for you.

You landed here from America, the country of eunuchs. You will collapse instantly and your blood will take a long time to empty out. No one will come to your aid. You will rot in the garbage dump.

I pray that Allah The Avenger will come to the aid of Qays, our young martyr from Tadjoura, so that he may accomplish his mission in all serenity. I am not too worried about him, for he received his training from Sheikh Aref, our best recruiter in this country.

As for me, tomorrow I will be another man. The day after tomorrow or some other day, soon. Our paths did not have the chance to meet one last time. And so be it. Allahu akbar!

●

The Day before the Night

No point denying it: fear never leaves me now. Fear makes my forehead burn, my temples sweat. I can't breathe. My hands, my legs . . . everything's trembling. I can see this fear migrating into people's furtive glances or into the silences that fall before the beginning of the curfew; since yesterday, it has been moved up to 6 p.m. It's really not the first time I have been accosted by fear but I must admit it hasn't left me for the past two days. There is no use vomiting up the contents of my guts, it sticks to my skin like a wet shirt. I refuse to tell Denise, at least for the moment. How could she help, from Montreal? I'll manage by myself, hold out for another twenty-four hours. If necessary I'll take refuge inside the security perimeter of an embassy. The French Consulate and the American Embassy aren't very far from my hotel. A five- or six-minute walk.

NOTEBOOK 4. SUNDAY, 8 OCTOBER. NOON.

Luckily, the fax machine in the hotel is working pretty well. I sent off the first results of my investigation to Denver by email from my computer and a fax to confirm. And if I have the time, I'll send an email to Denise to reassure her. The poor girl must be worried sick. Finally, I'll be leaving this evening if all goes well; if not, tomorrow at the latest. I am aware that the slightest last-minute obstacle could call everything into question. Ariel Klein, my boss's lawyer, warned me: it's all at my own risk now. If something happened to me, they won't lift a finger. Worse still, in their eyes I won't exist anymore. I am an unknown code, an outmoded programme to be thrown into the wastebasket with the click of a mouse.

NOTEBOOK 4. SUNDAY, 8 OCTOBER. 12.35 P.M.

By cross-checking various bits of information, I've reached the conclusion that this mysterious M. Aref is an agent with a checkered past. A native of Tadjoura, this former sergeant in the Djiboutian army was discharged after a sordid affair of corruption at the age of forty-six. He took a multitude of young men under his wing. They were attracted by violence, or relieved to get away from the depressing shores of unemployment. He crossed paths with Abshir before discretely leaving the country for Marseille where a very religious woman from the Comoros Islands became his second wife. Then he went up to Paris where he had easy access to a mosque on the outskirts of the city, attended by Islamist elements that the French counter-espionage agency identified as radicals. The spies of the Djibouti Embassy are closely monitoring his every move. He excels at recruiting and persuading fragile individuals. Reformed thugs, former drug addicts and failed artists are his most valued victims. His profile fits the testimony of the Frenchwoman, whom he had taken under his wing at the same time as an apparently harmless adolescent named Qays, like the famous poet of pre-Islamic times. Not much is known about Qays except that he's a young man who never got into any trouble. No police record or identification sheet. I was just able to learn that he had recently married a girl from his village. A local millionaire had offered a collective ceremony to thirty-odd couples; it took place in a big hotel under the obliging cameras of national television. This vast masquerade was organized just after the day of Eid ul-Fitr. This Qays individual must be totally insignificant or a religious fanatic to lend himself to such a sham.

●

_Ta_

O my false brother! I'm going to confide something in you for the very last time. Listen to me carefully if you have the time and if you're still in this world. It's not a confidence, really, but a rare sensation I've been experiencing. It has nothing to do with the ordinary course of things on this earth.

I cannot hide the fact that I feel a lump in my throat as I hold this parchment in my hands, for it is a parchment, even if it doesn't look like one. For a long time I thought I had a heap of loose pages, devoid of real evocative power. I also thought I would be able to get rid of those half-erased pages by covering them up with my own writing. I thought I could drown them in the sermons of my venerable Master and the floods of my black ink. I see now that I was overconfident; I was sure of my power, a bit like prostitutes who know they can pull any male into their sinful bed. But I hadn't reckoned with the power of the parchment. It is there, fresh and shining, resistant to humidity and soft to the touch, even though it is wavy and blistered in spots.

From that moment on, I knew my life would be taking an entirely different direction. Oh, not right away! Tomorrow afternoon, or some other day perhaps. The main thing is that the story of Walter Benjamin, the philosopher exiled in Paris, has found its way into my life, irrigating it with its underground charm. It has captivated me, or, better still, conquered me. For this story, I have neglected the repetitive commentaries of my Master. It doesn't matter who wrote it; this parchment has already enchanted me and has not yet revealed all its secrets. Meanwhile, I must remain silent. Otherwise my holy quest will have been annihilated before it barely began. And I can't even dare imagine my Master's reprimands and the punishments that would await me.

As soon as my venerable Master dozes off, I coddle my mysterious parchment, attracted by its smell of old paper, and its magic. Once you've gone through the first leaves, a veritable palimpsest is there before your eyes, like the heart of an artichoke. By going through its hawthorn pages with the most delicate attention, I discovered unexpected dwellers in them. Creatures both fragile and ancient. The leg of an insect, the petal of a rose, salt crystals and two white hairs set into the greasy texture of the vellum. Those are traces of the past. Tiny vestiges. What is the human brain if not a natural palimpsest? What is this book if not a homage to the human spirit and its immense aura?

If this book managed to reach me, it's because it was saved from destruction by other smugglers at each crucial period of its existence. I will be its decoder, its protector. The person who is its author, or at least its courier, may not be the man or woman who hid it in the hole I dug in the middle of our cell. It took some time to detect air holes in the ground no bigger than the tip of a little nail, and then hollow them out with my fingers. Luckily, cement eroded by iodine crumbles without too much difficulty.

I had to outwit the vigilance of my venerable Master again. But I realize that my Master might be aware of the existence of my treasure. Curious as he is, he must know how old this prison is and who the prisoners of former times were. Cultivated as he is, he must know the astonishing discovery of the Qumran

Manuscripts. Also called the Dead Sea Scrolls, that series of parchments and papyrus fragments found in earthenware jars in caves all around the site of Qumran, is a thousand years older than the oldest biblical text known to this day. By pure chance, in the spring of 1947, a simple Palestinian Bedouin named Mohammed Ahmed el-Hamed, who had gone out to look for one of his animals, fell upon these jars.

My venerable Master would not appreciate this discovery. He would wait for the right moment to put an end to my manoeuvres and send me to my death for treason.

I watch him with one eye, and as soon as he falls into a state of somnolence, I dig two centimetres deeper. Most often it makes me forget my earthly desires and those apocalyptic sermons. I have the feeling of being someone else, and his breath, the breath of a wild beast, is reaching my ears.

Today I can no longer keep the contents of this document to myself. It invited itself to me or, rather, imposed itself on me. I have this peculiar object in my hands. I will find a sanctuary for it so that it may be preserved after my death, if such is my destiny, and that is what counts. And if I should leave this prison alive, I will keep it right by me for the time I have left to live. My fate is still in the hands of Allah the Great Geometer, and that is how it should be . . .

The Book of Ben

. . . it all happened very fast at Portbou. The Spanish police refused to let old Ben through. A new directive, they said. Only people with an exit visa from France can cross the border. Absurd, replies Ben angrily. Turning these people back at the border means sending them back into the clutches of the Gestapo. In other words, sentence them to death.

Ben nearly collapses. From fatigue, from sheer disappointment. Illness, too, has been eating away at him for a long time. He is only forty-eight. He doesn't have the strength to turn back.

It is in a tiny room in the Fonda Francia hotel that he will write his last letter, taking away with him the burning enigmas of his life.

'In a situation with no way out, I have no other choice but to end it all. My life is going to end in a little village in the Pyrenees where no one knows me.

'Please give my best wishes to my friend Adorno and explain the situation in which I have now found myself. I don't have enough time left to write all the letters I would have liked to write.'

> Walter Benjamin to Henny Gurland
> (and Theodor W. Adorno?)
> Portbou, 25 September 1940

·

Epilogue

1170 Sunset Boulevard

Adorno Location Scouting HQ

Denver

Sunday, 8 October. 7.20 a.m.

The file named DD1 (Dubai/Djibouti 1) was faxed today at 12.15 p.m. local time from the lobby of the Sheraton Hotel to the main office of ALS (Adorno Location Scouting.)

The last page recapitulates in coded terms the handwritten recommendations of our agent. The last paragraph picks up the thread of the Frenchwoman's confession without further commentary, as if he did not have the time to refine this testimony and draw conclusions from it. Aside from that, this is a good, fairly detailed report, up to our professional standards.

Our agent Djib's body was found in a garbage dump right near Siesta Beach in Djibouti City. He had been knifed. He probably died from loss of blood. The local authorities have opened an investigation. Theft has been excluded as a motive, as the victim was not robbed. According to the information, still fragmentary at this stage, local intelligence agencies have a lead: they are focusing on the New Way, a terrorist organization well known to our agency.

Office of Global Logistics